# PREACHING
# LAW AND GOSPEL

# PREACHING LAW AND GOSPEL

## HERMAN G. STUEMPFLE, JR.

SIGLER PRESS   RAMSEY, NEW JERSEY

FIRST SIGLER PRESS EDITION 1991

*Library of Congress Cataloging-in-Publication Data*

Stuempfle, Herman G.
    Preaching Law and Gospel / Herman G. Stuempflle, Jr.
        p.        cm.
    Reprint, with new introd. Originally published:Philadelphia :
    Fortress Press, c1978
    Includes bibliographical references.
    ISBN 0-9623642-2-3
    1. Preaching. 2. Law and Gospel. I. Title.
[BV4211.2.S85    1990]                                    90-27268
    251--dc20                                                CIP

# CONTENTS

## Preface to Reprint Edition

Our potter son shocked his parents last year by destroying a collection of pieces which represented earlier stages of his work. He was embarrassed, he informed us, to have them seen. I have understood him better since, in preparation for a recent move, I was tempted to pack for the fourth time a collection of sermon manuscripts from the early years of my ministry. I resisted and consigned them to overdue oblivion.

Every preacher understands that. There's a certain datedness, if not obsolescence, about what we preached at another time in another place. Seldom can an old sermon be used again without major alterations to make it fit more closely some present situation.

Though books are not quite as transient as sermons, they do not altogether escape time's erosion of their currency. The present volume is no exception. It was written in the mid 1970's and was based on a dissertation presented in the late 1960's. Those years were not a heartening time for preachers. The pulpit, along with every other feature of the local parish, was charged with being irrelevant to the church's mission in a secularized society. Hence, the original preface of this volume rehearsed the dismal evidence for the malaise which preachers were experiencing.

i

As we enter the last decade of the twentieth century, the mood with respect to preaching has changed significantly. No longer does the first week of an introductory homiletics class need to be devoted to an *apologia* for the importance of the preaching office. Seminarians assume that the Sunday sermon will be a central and critical instrument of their ministry among working pastors. They eagerly attend continuing education events on preaching and gather with their peers to work together on the coming Sunday's appointed texts. They buy "proclamation aids" from church publishing houses to assist them in the faithful interpretation of Scripture. They recognize their responsibility to be "servants of the Word" to their people who, incidentally, had never lost their expectation that strong preaching should lie at the heart of a parish pastor's ministry.

In light of this changed context, would I write this volume differently, had I the opportunity? I hope it does not sound presumptuous to say that I would not. I continue to hold to its fundamental thesis, that "whatever other elements contribute to the making of a sermon, there is a certain theological substructure which is indispensable." Likewise, no doubt because of a theological heritage which I cannot and feel no need to abandon, I continue to see that theological foundation most adequately described in the classic Reformation categories of Law and Gospel.

If rewriting were an option, I would, however, give further attention to two sections of this study. First, I would try harder to clarify the relationship between the preaching of Law as "hammer of judgement" and the preaching of Law as "mirror of existence." There is, I still believe, a helpful distinction to be made between the two modes, but they must be distinguished in a way that does not undercut the biblical diagnosis of humanity's deepest malady as sin, for which

God's justifying grace in Christ is the only cure. Some readers of this book felt that this point was not made with sufficient strength.

Second, I would want to do more research into the relationship between justifiction and sanctification, the Gospel's promise and its ethical consequences. The questions which cluster here are as old as the Reformers' debates over a possible "third use of the Law." The chapter on "The Call to Obedience" is my effort, in light of what I knew then, to deal with this issue as it relates to preaching. Though I would not substantially change what I wrote, the decade since has made me aware that there are more complexities to be probed on this topic. Unfortunately, that same decade has not afforded me time to conduct such an exploration. Perhaps some new reader will take up that needed work.

One of the shocks experienced in rereading an old sermon or book derives from the recognition of one's obtuse-ness with respect to linguistic inclusivity. We sound as though we worshipped a masculine deity in an all-male world! Fortunately, our eyes and ears have, at least to some degree, been opened since those cavalier days. I wish I could push some "correct" button to immediately change every exclusive "him" or "his" in this manuscript to language that would include my sister clergy and laity. Since such amend-ments aren't possible in a reprint, I can only hope that those most affected will accept my apologies and believe my assurance that I've learned better since.

Finally, I express gratitude to Sigler Press for making this reprint possible. I hope their judgement that it can continue to contribute to the health of preaching in the church will prove true.

Gettysburg, Pennsylvania
September, 1990

# PREFACE

Though my present place of ministry in the church does not require of me a weekly sermon, I still count myself a working member of the guild of preaching clergy. Furthermore, my memories of those parish days when Sunday morning came round with inexorable regularity are still vivid. The mix of joy and anguish which attended the weekly event of preaching—both in the hours of preparation and in the minutes of delivery—has shaped in profound ways my self-consciousness both as person and as pastor.

My ministry of preaching has included years during which the pulpit was under frontal attack. The parish was being written off as an obsolete form of Christian life and mission. Since preaching, at least in most Protestant communions, had long held center stage in congregational life, it was a particularly vulnerable target for such critique. If the parish was defunct, then preaching—either as cause or effect—had to share that fate.

There was at that time no end to the voices confirming such a negative verdict. Most writers in the field of homiletics felt obliged to preface what they had to say concerning preaching with doleful words about its present state and future prospects. Sociologists cited evidence that people who regularly listened to sermons scored, in terms of the ethical quality of their daily actions and attitudes, about the same as or even a little lower than those who never went near a church.

All of this did little to bolster the sagging self-image of those of us who had been taught that we were ordained primarily to be preachers of the Word and administrators of the sacraments. The sacraments were at least visible acts, but what of those ephemeral puffs of air that seemed to die somewhere between our lips and our people's ears? We wondered out loud whether the time required to prepare and preach a sermon was worth it. Furthermore, if we were listening attentively to the dominant "Word of God" theologies of the day, we sensed a bewildering incongruity between the theological claims advanced on behalf of preaching and its apparently miniscule effects in the actual life of the church. Obviously, more was being claimed for it theologically than preaching seemed able to deliver experientially.

Many reasons were advanced to explain this depressing gap between theory and actuality. Some pointed to an erosion of the theological resources of those of us who preached, so that the Sunday sermon was often essentially uninformed by the central affirmations of the Christian tradition. Others placed the blame on a severing of the cord which links the pulpit to Scripture, with a consequent loss of homiletical nourishment from the biblical kerygma. Still others, drawing upon insights from the field of communication theory, exposed significant "barriers to communication" in the language and form of the sermon and in the setting of the preaching event.

All of us who preach in the church will recognize the accuracy of these diagnoses. The re-examination which preaching, along with other elements in parish life, has as a result been forced to undergo has been both painful and helpful. Many of us have been driven to a recovery of vital roots in Scripture and theology, even as we have gained new understanding of ways by which the sermon, as a form of inter-human communication, can be made more effective. As a result, the pulpit appears not merely to have survived the assaults of the recent past but to be undergoing renewal.

Many of us are encouraged to see it again as that point in the weekly rhythm of parish life where what the Reformers called the "living voice of the Gospel" resounds.

My hope is that the chapters which follow will contribute to the continuing renewal of the pulpit. They reflect my conviction that while preaching is by no means the only mode by which the Gospel is communicated in the life of the church, it is and will continue to be the central mode. We who are called to the ministry of Word and sacraments will continue to see the Sunday sermon as potentially our most fruitful opportunity for addressing our people with the claim of the Word of God. We will approach our task, therefore, with appropriate seriousness and expectation.

The most direct source of this book is my doctoral dissertation, prepared for the faculty of the School of Theology at Claremont, California. In its present form it is considerably abridged and revised. I want, however, to express appreciation to Professors K. Morgan Edwards, John B. Cobb, Rolf B. Knierim and Allen J. Moore, who served as my committee at that earlier stage and who encouraged me to continue my work on the topic then and now under consideration. I am deeply grateful also to the Ecumenical Institute, Collegeville, Minnesota, for a summer fellowship which provided the quiet setting in which the first draft of this manuscript could be written.

In addition to the direct source just mentioned, this book, like all books, has been fed by innumerable other tributaries, many of them hidden from the consciousness of the author himself. Sermons heard and preached over many years, pastoral experiences, books read, conversations with friends and colleagues, class sessions with students—these items and many more form the streams emptying into the main channel of concern out of which a book such as this emerges. But of one of those tributaries I am fully conscious—the preaching of my father, whose sermons are the earliest in my memory and in whose words I first heard *the* Word of God's judgment and mercy. To his memory this book is now dedicated.

# -1-

# THE THEOLOGICAL FOUNDATIONS
# OF THE SERMON

Many elements go into the making of a sermon. No less than poets and painters we preachers must be willing to submit ourselves to the exacting discipline of an artistic form. We cannot preach without devoting attention to such matters as language, structure, design, imagery, and delivery. The fact that the sermon relies ultimately upon the power of the Holy Spirit for its vitality does not relieve us in our preaching from penultimate responsibility for careful craftsmanship. But along with this attention to the sermon as sermon, it is essential that we develop equal skill in discerning the theological realities which undergird our own work. I am persuaded that whatever other elements contribute to the making of a sermon, there is a certain theological substructure which is indispensable.

## THEOLOGY AND THE SERMON

Systematic theologians, especially those in the Barthian tradition, have taken pains to define carefully the relationship between their vocation and that of the preacher. They see theology and preaching existing in a symbiotic relationship. Theology, on its side, has no reason to exist except to serve the church in its task of proclaiming the Gospel. The past proclamation of the church provides material upon which the theologian reflects. The future proclamation of

11

the church is the object of the theologian's concern. Out of systematic investigation of the Word which the church has already proclaimed the theologian struggles to articulate norms for preaching still to be done. Thus theologians will often confront preachers in the role of critic. They must hold preachers accountable for the Word they presume to utter from the pulpit: Have you been faithful to the tradition of which Scripture is the primary witness? Have the words of your sermon given expression to that unique Word of which you as preacher are the servant, or have they merely been echoes of voices from your own psyche or the surrounding culture? By raising such questions, theology serves as "the conscience of preaching."[1]

It is fatal, however, if we lay the whole burden of theological reflection about our preaching upon the shoulders of the professional theologian. Preachers who demur that they are "not theologians" cannot, by that disclaimer, absolve themselves of responsibility for the theological content of the Sunday sermon. Nothing is more certain than the fact that *some* theology will surface in every sermon. The danger is that it will do so without prior reflection, uncorrected by the great tradition in which all of us preachers stand and of which we are in some sense "guardians." Unintended "theologies" will begin to dominate our preaching and to distort or even subvert the distinctive Word we are called to proclaim. When we take time to subject our past preaching to theological analysis, we may be astounded to discover that we have been purveying such strange doctrines as the perfectibility of man and society in history, the immortality of the soul, or the demand to justify oneself before God by moral or spiritual achievement.

## TWO THEOLOGICAL SCHEMA

Two contemporary writers in the field of homiletics have provided preachers with particularly useful schematizations which can serve as a framework for theological reflection on our task. The first, by Kyle Haselden, is inductive in nature, taking its cues from the examination of a large body of sermonic material. The second, by Heinrich Ott, is deductive, starting from one of the major confessional documents of the Protestant tradition.

Kyle Haselden claims that his analysis of sermons from the whole range of the history of Christian preaching reveals three indispensable elements in what he characterizes as "the good sermon . . . the biblical sermon." These elements are: (1) a description of and warning about "man's peril," (2) an announcement of "God's promise" standing over against our threatened situation, and (3) the proclamation of "God's act" in Christ which gives effect to the promise.[2] The preacher should pose to himself two questions as he seeks to determine the theological integrity of any sermon: "Does the sermon warn man of the danger in which sin and mortality submerge his whole being? Does the sermon hold out to such a man the promise of God's redeeming and resurrecting love?"[3] In short, a trinity of peril-promise-agent should reach expression in every Christian sermon.

Haselden further declares that this threefold scheme reflects a pattern present in great imaginative works of literature. His thesis is confirmed if you overlay his scheme upon a novel like Camus' *The Plague*: The peril is the bubonic plague which is laying waste a city in North Africa. The promise is the availability of a limited supply of medicine and the hope that the disease will run its course before the city is decimated. The agent is Dr. Rieux, a courageous physician who against all odds stays at his post ministering to the stricken populace.

It should be observed, however, that in much contemporary literature the third element in Haselden's trinity is missing. In Samuel Beckett's *Waiting for Godot*, for example, the peril is the meaninglessness, emptiness, and mutual hostility which threaten to engulf two tramps, Vladimir and Estragon. The promise is an ambiguous announcement that a mysterious figure named Godot is coming to deliver them. The play ends, however, with Godot nowhere in sight and without even the assurance that he actually exists.

But it is precisely the coming of the redemptive Agent

that lies at the center of the Christian drama. The announcement of Jesus' entrance upon the stage of our history and
his death and resurrection there certify to us the promise
that we are not abandoned in our peril. This is the essence
of the Word we are called to preach, and Haselden's analysis
is a vivid way of holding it before us. Furthermore, since
the Gospel is more accurately described as story or drama
than as dogma or doctrine his schematization is appropriately dynamic in its quality. It is suggestive not only of the
content a Christian sermon should hold but also of the form
in which it should be cast. A sermon should have more of
the marks of a narrative than of an essay.[4]

The second analysis of the theological substructure of the
sermon is by Heinrich Ott. His starting point is the Heidelberg Catechism which in its three main parts touches upon:
(1) man's "sin and wretchedness," (2) the "redemption"
wrought on our behalf by God through Christ, and (3) the
obligations of gratitude which God's redeeming act lays
upon us.

These three elements, Ott maintains, correspond to the
"structural phases" of the life of faith. In the first phase we
are brought to the realization that our situation before God
is one of "lostness." Then through the Word of Jesus' redemptive work we experience, in the midst of our lost situation, an emancipating encounter with God. Finally, out of
this encounter there issues a radical reorientation of our life
toward new ends.

Ott insists that each of these "structural phases" of the
life of faith is to have a parallel element in the sermon. On
the one side, the sermon must speak realistically and con-
vincingly about our human predicament. On the other side,
it must speak concretely about the quality of life to which
those claimed by God's grace are obligated. But in the
center, forming the theological heartbeat of all preaching,
there must be the clear and joyous announcement that in
Jesus Christ God has come to us for our help.

Actual sermons will not follow this scheme in any wooden

way. The balance among the three elements will be conditioned by the biblical text and by the actualities of the particular preaching situation. The order of the points will be rearranged and will interpenetrate each other; nevertheless,

> . . . in principle the sermon as a whole has just these three things to say. Its centre lies in the middle point, in the proclamation of God's action. But in order to be intelligible and effective, this proclamation needs the other two parts, the disclosure of the true situation and the emphasis on the resulting obligation.[5]

## LAW AND GOSPEL

Clearly, both Haselden and Ott are rooted in the classic theology of the Reformation. Ott calls attention to this fact by allowing the Heidelberg Catechism to provide the source material from which he constructs the theology by which the contemporary sermon should be informed. While Haselden is not so explicit in identifying his heritage, there is no mistaking the congruence of his peril-promise-agent scheme with the familiar Reformation categories of Law and Gospel. His insistence that preaching must sound the alarm to people trapped in a situation of radical threat is nothing other than the Reformers' conviction that God's Law must be proclaimed with all its power to convict persons of sin. His equal insistence that preaching must announce a Word of promise, of which Jesus is God's Agent, is only another way of stating the Reformers' recovery of the truth of God's justifying grace offered to sinners in Jesus Christ.

It is to be noted that Ott's third point, that preaching should hold before its hearers the obligations of gratitude for God's act of grace, reveals his rootage in the Reformed wing of the sixteenth-century Reformation. This formulation raises the complex question of the "third use of the Law," to which we will have occasion to return later. Put briefly, those who stand in the Lutheran tradition have generally defined the role of the Law in terms of "accuser," acting prior to justification, while those in the Calvinist lineage have seen the Law additionally in the role of "guide," directing our life following justification.

For Luther especially, the categories of Law and Gospel were theologically central and decisive. A portion of the following chapters will be devoted to an examination of each of these categories in his thought as they relate to the task of preaching. Here, to provide a context for that discussion, it will be useful to review briefly his doctrine of the twofold form of the Word of God.

## THE TWOFOLD FORM OF THE
## WORD OF GOD

It is clear that the resurgent "Word of God" theologies of the twentieth century have their most direct roots in Luther. At the center of his thought stands the God who addresses us with his Word. God is the One who again and again breaks the silence of eternity and speaks to us. In fact, Luther's whole theology has been characterized as a "theology of the Word of God."[6]

This concentration upon "the God who speaks" is the correlate of Luther's insistence that we have no direct access to the mystery of God's essential being, that is, to "the absolute God." God in himself is infinitely beyond our reach. In fact, the "unclothed God" would overwhelm and destroy us in the awesomeness of his glory. We must rather lay hold of the God who comes to us "not naked but clothed and revealed in his Word."[7]

But just as we cannot know God in his essential being, neither can we know him in his primal unity. The revealing Word addresses us in twofold form—stereophonically, one might say, rather than monophonically. God speaks as both the God of wrath and the God of mercy, and so sharp is the tension between these two roles that he often seems to be two gods rather than the one God. Yet it is indeed one God who addresses us, exercising through wrath and judgment his "alien work" and through grace and forgiveness his "proper work." It is by his Word as Law that God executes his "alien work" and by his Word as Gospel that he accomplishes his "proper work."

In his early writings Luther followed the scholastics in distinguishing between the "old law" of the Old Testament and the "new law" (Gospel) of the New Testament. Later, however, he draws the dividing line not between the two testaments but between two radically different modes of God's Word to us. Each can be heard in *both* testaments. In fact, the same text can function as both Law and Gospel. The First Commandment, for example, can condemn us for our idolatries, but in its clear affirmation of God's sovereignty it can also provide a secure foundation for our trust.[8]

It is not in Scripture but in preaching that the distinction between Law and Gospel becomes most crucially important. For all his praise of Scripture, Luther never tires in declaring the primacy of the Word preached from a human mouth to a living congregation. The church is a "mouth house" rather than a "pen house,"[9] even as the New Testament Gospel was preached before it was written down. As a summons for persons to repent and believe, the Word's natural and proper form is spoken. The oral proclamation of the sermon is the means by which God addresses persons in the present moment with both his Word of judgment and his Word of grace.

This is why preachers must be adept at distinguishing between Law and Gospel. It is through their living voices that God addresses his people either to afflict or to comfort, and it is a great art to know which form of the Word is needed and how it is to be spoken. Any confusion of the two forms results in the collapse of both. If the Law is robbed of its power to expose our utter bankruptcy before God, then our predicament is not extreme and the Word of grace is unnecessary. If, on the other hand, the Gospel is presented as in any sense a new demand laid upon us, then our situation is indeed hopeless for there remains no other Word to release us from our already impossible burden. The first error leads people into the false security of self-righteousness; the second plunges them into the abyss of despair. Either way, the result is detrimental to the possibility of a right relationship with God in which his grace and our faith live in dynamic interaction.

Yet Luther had no illusion that to distinguish between Law and Gospel is an easy task. Separable in terms of theological analysis, they are nevertheless very closely joined in experience.[10] They lie interlaced with each other in the same human heart, for the Christian is always at the same time "sinner and justified." Therefore, we never hear the promise of the Gospel without, insofar as we are still "in the flesh," hearing also the rumbling threats of the Law. Nor do we hear the threats of the Law without, insofar as we are also "in the Spirit," rejoicing in the promise of forgiveness announced to us in the Gospel. This human difficulty in separating experientially what can be readily divided theologically led Luther to conclude:

> There's no man living on earth who knows how to distinguish between the Law and the Gospel. We may think we understand it when we're listening to a sermon, but we're far from it. Only the Holy Spirit knows this. Even the man Christ was so wanting in understanding when he was in the vineyard that an angel had to console him. . . . Because I've been writing so long about it, you'd think I'd know the distinction, but when the crisis comes I recognize very well that I am far, far from understanding. So God alone should and must be our holy master.[11]

## NOTES

1. Heinrich Ott, *Theology and Preaching* (Philadelphia: Westminster Press, 1965), p. 22.

2. Kyle Haselden, *The Urgency of Preaching* (New York: Harper & Row, 1963), p. 42.

3. Ibid., p. 55.

4. For a stimulating discussion of the story or parabolic nature of the Christian message see Sallie McFague TeSelle, *Speaking in Parables: A Study in Metaphor and Theology* (Philadelphia: Fortress Press, 1975).

5. Ott, *Theology and Preaching*, p. 53.

6. Jaroslav Pelikan, "Luther the Expositor," in *Luther's Works,* ed. Jaroslav Pelikan and Helmut T. Lehmann (St. Louis: Concordia Press; Philadelphia: Fortress Press, 1955–), 30a:48 (hereafter cited as *LW*).

7. Martin Luther, "Commentary on Psalm 45" (1533–1534), *LW* 12:312.

8. Pelikan, "Luther the Expositor," *LW* 30a:66.

9. Martin Luther, "Church Postil" (1522), quoted in Regin Prenter, "Luther on Word and Sacrament," in *More About Luther* (Decorah, Iowa: Luther College Press, 1958), p. 73.

10. Luther contends that human nature is such that, in actual experience, "the Gospel is a rare guest but the Law a constant guest" in the conscience (Martin Luther, "Lectures on Galatians" [1535], *LW* 26:117).

11. Martin Luther, "Table Talk" (1531), *LW* 54:127·

# –2–

# LAW:
# HAMMER OF JUDGMENT AND
# MIRROR OF EXISTENCE

John Steinbeck in *Travels with Charley* reports a Sunday morning visit to a small, clapboard church in a Vermont village:

> The minister, a man of iron with tool-steel eyes and a delivery like a pneumatic drill, opened up with a prayer and reassured us that we were a pretty sorry lot. . . . Then, having softened us up, he went into a glorious sermon. Having proved that we, or perhaps only I, were no damn good, he painted with cool certainty what was likely to happen to us if we didn't make some basic reorganizations for which he didn't hold out much hope. He spoke of hell as an expert, not the mush-mush hell of these soft days, but a well-stoked, white hot hell served by technicians of the first order.[1]

Such an image, along with hazy impressions of Jonathan Edwards and his "Sinners in the Hands of an Angry God,"[2] is what most people associate with the preaching of Law. It is preaching which makes a relentless, not to say ruthless, attack upon the conscience. The tradition, in the history of Christian preaching, runs from Peter, whose sermon at Pentecost is reported to have "cut to the heart" of his listeners, to Billy Graham in a Madison Square Garden crusade. It is a mode of preaching the Law which we will characterize, bor-

20

rowing a symbol from Luther, as "the hammer of judgment." But in this chapter we will also speak of another mode of preaching the Law which we will describe, borrowing a phrase from Tillich, as "the mirror of existence."

## THE LAW AS HAMMER
## OF JUDGMENT

Both Haselden and Ott, as we have seen, insist upon a place in the theological scheme of the sermon for the preaching of Law. Haselden speaks of warning about the "danger in which sin and mortality submerge [our] whole being"; Ott, of the "sin and wretchedness" which are the ineradicable marks of our life in this world. It is essential, they would contend, for the preacher to expose the unvarnished truth about our condition. There must be no touching up of the human portrait so as to hide the multiple ways in which we have defaced our true personhood. The sermon must not relieve the sense of crisis which is appropriate to our actual situation but must awaken and intensify it.

Since Paul, Christian preachers have spoken about our human crisis predominantly in terms of sin and guilt. The preaching of the Law has been aimed at the activation of the conscience. When Paul described the Law as a *paidogogos* or tutor (Gal. 3:24) he did not have in mind a kindly pedagogue of the "Mr. Chips" variety. The *paidogogos* in Paul's world was a special slave, notable for his severity, whose function was to threaten and punish the boys in his charge. It has been suggested that "chastiser" or "custodian" is the most adequate translation.[3] The Law, in Paul's view, stands before us like an implacable enemy.

This harsh definition of the Law dominates Luther's thought. Medieval theology had spoken of "sin, death, and the devil" as mankind's chief foes. Luther added to that list the Law and God's wrath. Though the Law as an expression of the will of a good God can only be good itself, yet for fallen creatures it has been transformed into a terrifying tyrant barring our way to God. Incapable of fulfilling the Law's demands, we nevertheless engage in a self-defeating struggle to win God's favor by keeping it. Thus our plight is compounded, and the Law which God intended as a blessing has become a curse. Luther employs an array of graphic images to portray the futility of our efforts to storm heaven by keeping the Law. We are like Sisyphus eternally pushing a huge boulder to the top of a hill only to watch it roll to the bottom again.[4] In all our struggling to move forward, we only make "crab's progress," that is, we go sideways.[5] We are like a man who tries to clean himself by washing with dirt.[6] Or we are like one beggar trying to help another, as in the old proverb in which "one of these is milking a billy goat and the other is holding the sieve."[7]

Actually, Luther posits two "uses" of the Law in the economy of God's dealing with mankind. The first he calls the "political use." Here the Law functions primarily as a restraint upon human wickedness to prevent the world from degenerating into a jungle of self-destructive violence. It operates through the "orders" of society, primarily the state, and controls the unruly passions of men by threat of punishment.

The primary use of the Law in Luther's thought, however, is the "theological use." Here God's demand is deepened. The "civil righteousness" of constrained obedience to external authority will no longer do. What is required is the "inner righteousness" of pure, joyous love toward God and neighbor. But since we have an inveterate tendency to evade facing up to both the depth of God's demand upon us and our failure to meet it, the Law becomes God's instrument for awakening us to our true situation. Prone as we are to smug self-righteousness, "God has to send some Hercules, the Law, to attack, subdue, and destroy this monster with full force."[8] The Law is a "large and powerful hammer"[9] with which God smashes our pretentions and brings us to our knees. In this way, we are finally driven to recognize the desperateness of our condition and to cry out for help. Thus, the Law can be "a most useful servant impelling us to Christ."[10]

Two characteristics stand out in Luther's view of the "theological use" of the Law. First, the Law falls upon us vertically, intersecting our lives as a demand and/or threat from God himself. It is true that preachers are the mouthpiece on earth of God's Word as Law, and they are not to be remiss in the office of rebuking in the church;[11] but God himself is ultimately the wielder of this "large and powerful hammer" of judgment. He is the source of the Law and the One who speaks through the lips of his preachers.

Second, the target of this hammer of judgment is the conscience. God's Word as Law addresses us primarily at that point in our existence where such terms as freedom and responsibility have relevance. It holds us accountable for the condition of our lives. "The Law always accuses. . . ."[12] It backs us into a corner from which there is no escape and finally evokes from us a plea of "guilty."

THE LAW AS MIRROR
OF EXISTENCE

It is easy to hear in Luther's understanding of Law echoes of his own anguished question, "How can I find a gracious God?" Luther spoke for an age in which people defined the crisis of their lives primarily in categories of guilt and forgiveness.

Preaching whose Law dimension focuses upon our culpability before God is in a direct line of succession with this tradition represented by Luther. But there are those who deny its relevance for our modern world. It must be asked whether Luther's question (not really different from Paul's fifteen centuries earlier), "How can I find a gracious God?" speaks authentically for the present generation. Clearly there are many people today to whom it would never occur to begin a definition of their situation with a confession of guilt before God. Indeed, in the age of "the death of God," the reality of God is itself for many at best a question. When the vertical dimension has simply collapsed as part of their understanding of life it is unlikely that talk of accountability to a demanding, judging God will claim their attention.

This shift in our contemporary consciousness is reflected in certain more recent theological interpretations of the meaning of Law. Paul Tillich, for example, offers this description of our fundamental human situation: "The state of existence is the state of estrangement. Man is estranged from the ground of being, from other beings, and from himself."[13] It should be noted that the word *estrangement* in itself suggests nothing whatsoever about our responsibility, or lack of it, for our condition. It is morally neutral. While not necessarily closed to the question of guilt, the word *estrangement* is in fact one of a cluster of terms drawn from existentialist literature to define what Tillich calls the "structures of existence." This cluster includes such terms as *alienation, meaninglessness, brokenness, finitude, anxiety* and *despair.* The question of human accountability may lurk in their depths, but it is not immediately visible on the surface.

Ott argues that such terms as the above may be much more useful to the contemporary preacher than the traditional language of sin and guilt. Existentialist categories such as "homelessness," "decadence," and "existence in unreality" may carry modern man "a real step forward in the recognition of the essential truth" about himself and "therefore be a real help homiletically."[14] "Existence in unreality," for example, points to the nature of life bereft of God, and this very emptiness of existence in separation from God is a sign of judgment. Though contemporary listeners may not at first interpret their plight with any reference to God, it is our task as preachers to bring them at last to an awareness of the full theological implication of what they experience only as unreality, hollowness, or emptiness. When the Law is thus understood in terms of a description of the actualities of our existence in this world, it is no longer "a special aspect or theme of proclamation, but its entire, all-embracing horizon."[15] It is a theme in a minor mode which continually resounds in the sermon to inform it with a realism in which people will recognize the contours of life as they know it.

Such an analysis represents a shift from the Reformation tradition with respect to the Law and its use in preaching.

It illuminates the fact that the sickness we carry in the roots of our being is describable not only as guilt but includes such symptoms as doubt, alienation, and despair, about which it is possible to speak in descriptive rather than accusatory terms. They are aspects of what Tillich calls life on "the boundary situation," and it is part of the function of preaching to lay bare this situation with such clarity that it will be impossible for us to escape into any of the false secular or religious securities which beckon us.

It is possible to summarize this recent interpretation of Law by again highlighting two characteristics. First, the stress falls upon the horizontal dimension of the Law's operation rather than upon the vertical. Judgment is not so much an attack from above as a threat from within the actualities of our life. It is the "reality of fallen man," "man's being as it in fact is."[16]  There is no explicit reference here to God as the Source of the Law's demand or as the Accuser whose searching Word backs us into a corner. The Law is something given within the structures of our existence, functioning without the intervention of a divine Giver.

Second, the target of the Law is not so much the conscience as, more broadly, our consciousness of the true situation in which we stand. The function of the Law is not so much to accuse as to expose. Preachers of the Law do not speak only—and usually not immediately—of our moral responsibility. They seek first to open our eyes rather than to bring us to our knees. If Luther's "hammer" is an appropriate symbol for the classic interpretation of the Law, then a helpful image for this contemporary interpretation is provided in these words of Tillich:

What we must do, and can do successfully, is to show the structures of anxiety, of conflicts, of guilt. These structures, which are effective because they mirror what we are, are in us, and if we are right, they are in other people also. If we bring these structures before them, then it is as if we held up *a mirror in which they see themselves.*[17]

## PREACHING LAW TODAY

The two interpretations of Law we have considered can be outlined as follows:

|  | HAMMER OF JUDGMENT | MIRROR OF EXISTENCE |
|---|---|---|
| Function | accusation | description |
| Target | conscience | consciousness |
| Goal | accountability | awareness |
| Symptom (s) | guilt | anxiety, finitude, alienation, doubt, despair |

It should be stated that the purpose of this analysis has not been to set one mode of viewing Law over against the other. Law as "hammer" and Law as "mirror" are not mutually contradictory. Indeed, Tillich himself argues strongly for the retention of the word *sin* in the Christian vocabulary to point up the fact that, while our condition of estrangement has a tragic and universal character, it also includes a moral dimension for which we must bear responsibility.[18] Furthermore, any comprehensive description of the human condition will finally include, along with the other symptoms listed under the second column above, the reality of guilt. This too is an aspect of "man's being as it in fact is." Thus Law as "hammer of judgment" and Law as "mirror of existence" should be seen as complementary modes of preaching Law. The more contemporary interpretation does not negate the older tradition but raises to a new prominence accents in the proclamation of Law which have received only limited attention in the Reformation heritage.

Against this background it is possible now to sketch three guidelines for the preaching of Law today and to provide some illustrations from actual sermons.

1. *We will preach Law today in order to confront those who hear with their accountability for their lives.*

This guideline implies a conviction that Luther's question, "How can I find a gracious God?" is not obsolete as an evocation of our human dilemma. There are many persons in our parishes for whom the categories of sin and guilt are vigorously, even destructively, alive. That some of them are persons for whom the experience of guilt is neurotic and pathological is obvious. For these therapy may be more immediately helpful than preaching. But there are many who, acknowledging their freedom and responsibility before God, know that an irremovable question mark hovers above them. They cannot justify what they have made of their lives. For these the preaching of Law as judgment will be a help in clarifying the source and shape of their guilt. For all of us, granted our incurable bias toward self-justification and our gift for rationalizing away the wrong that is in us, this classic mode of preaching the Law serves as a necessary alarm bell to awaken us from fateful sleep.

A passage from a sermon by Edmund Steimle illustrates the preaching of Law as judgment. He creates an analogy in which we are landlords and God is a prospective tenant:

> I welcome him into the house of my soul, of course, so long as he observes my house rules. I want it understood that I want no discomfort or disturbance in the way I run my life. I don't want to change my habits; if I have a few prejudices I don't intend to change them. I shall expect a reasonable amount of "peace of mind"; I don't want to lie awake nights worrying about the problems of the world or the state of my own soul; I have worries enough as it is. If God wants to move into my house under those conditions, I'll be more than happy to have him . . .[19]

Several clues about the effective preaching of Law as judgment emerge from that brief passage. The preacher does not talk about sin in general but is specific and concrete in exposing the self-deceptions to which we are prone. Yet while singling out particular manifestations of sin, for example prejudice or complacency, he traces them back to the root evil of our proud autonomy before God and neighbor.

Furthermore, if a "hammer" is used here it is less like a heavy sledge than the mallet with which a detective sounds for a hollow panel in a wall.  The listener therefore is not put so quickly on the defensive but is invited to participate with the preacher in an act of self-examination.  This effect is heightened by the consistent use of the first person pronoun.  The Word of judgment is cast in the form of a confessional so that the preacher is clearly seen to be a participant in the guilt he describes.

The passage just cited exposes the more interior motions of sin.  In preaching Law today, however, we will also address our common involvement in the social ills of our time.  There is a "solidarity of all" in responsibility for poverty and hunger, environmental blight, malfunctions of government, and the ultimate violence of war.  No matter how remote we may seem to be from the nerve centers of society, the preaching of Law must help us see the threads both of action and of apathy which link us to the massive national and global crises of this century.

An example of such preaching appears in the following excerpt from a college baccalaureate sermon by John Vannorsdall:

> All of you will very soon live in at least three rooms, have at least one good suit or dress, more than one pair of shoes, eat some kind of meat at least twice a day, have your own transportation, and be protected against sickness and old age. The problem is not your own poverty, but how to enjoy your meat while a man, his wife, and his children stand outside peering through your window, hungry and cold.
>
> This is the risk which you took when you accepted the invitation to walk in the way of insight—the risk of learning that these people are there; the risk of knowing that you are a part of that small number who enjoy the basic necessities of life. You've learned that the haunted faces of the "have-nots" reveal a restlessness, that they know of your relative wealth, and that they lay claim to basic necessities as fellow human beings.  They will not longer "have not."
>
> You could, perhaps, have rejoiced in simpleness, in the traditional tale that people are lazy, lacking intelligence, and

destined to their lot.  Or you might have worn those strange
glasses which allow us to see the greater wealth of the man
next door but will not let us see the faces pressed against our
own window . . . [But] having lost your simpleness, you are
now destined to eat your bread in the face of the hungry;
destined to be torn by their cry for help and by your own
unwillingness and seeming incapacity to do much about it.[20]

Note the way in which the preacher forces us to see our
inescapable solidarity with the poor and the dispossessed.
The direct second person form of address prevents us from
escaping our own presence in the scene he projects.  He also
vividly personalizes the plight of the hungry so that the
human face of suffering is not lost in the cold abstraction of
a statistic.  The moral dilemma of our relative wealth is
pressed upon us in a way that forces us to examine our attitudes and to ask what we must do.

2. *We will preach Law today in order to bring those who
   hear to a heightened consciousness of the dark underside of their existence.*

For this mode of preaching Law "the mirror of existence"
is a more appropriate symbol than "the hammer of judgment."  There are many—and they may form a majority in
the contemporary world—for whom guilt is not the primary
category by which they define their situation.  They resonate
more immediately to such terms as meaninglessness, anxiety,
despair, or alienation.  Furthermore even where guilt is a
dominant element in experience it is not the sole one.  If we
cast the Law dimension of our sermons only in terms of sin
and guilt, we miss those who do not see themselves first of
all as sinners and neglect areas of experience which are
vividly real even for those who do.

Two examples of the preaching of Law in this mode will
help clarify what is meant.  The first is from an Ash Wednes-
day sermon by H. A. Williams entitled "The True Wilderness" and is based upon the account of Jesus' temptation.

The "wilderness" becomes for Williams a richly-freighted image which carries the reality of our own inner world:

> . . . the wilderness belongs to us. It is always lurking somewhere as part of our experience, and there are times when it seems pretty near the whole of it. . . . Most people's wilderness is inside them, not outside. Thinking of it as outside is only a trick we play on ourselves—a trick to hide from us what we really are, not comfortingly wicked, but incapable, for the time being, of establishing communion. Our wilderness, then, is an inner isolation. It's an absence of contact. It's a sense of being alone—boringly alone, or saddeningly alone, or terrifyingly alone. Often we try to relieve it—understandably enough, God knows—by chatter, or gin, or religion, or sex, or possibly a combination of all four. The trouble is that these . . . can work their magic only for a very limited time, leaving us after one short hour or two exactly where we were before.[21]

Here the preacher sets out not to accuse us but to evoke our self-recognition. His aim is not to make us feel guilty but to encourage us to remove the masks behind which we hide our real faces from ourselves and others. The consequence may not be the confession that we are "by nature sinful and unclean" but rather the acknowledgment that at the deepest levels of our lives we are anxious, broken, and lonely. We listen and sense that, along with the preacher, we too have been there in the wilderness. We are drawn, not driven, to self-recognition as we see our own lives mirrored in the words of the sermon.

When we proclaim the Law effectively in this mode, we are accomplishing through the homiletical form what the creative artists of our time are doing through their forms. We are holding up an "image of man" which has power to awaken self-awareness. In fact, the best contemporary art forms frequently suggest evocative symbols which we can employ in the Law dimension of the sermon. One preacher who does this with great sensitivity is Charles Rice. In his volume, *Interpretation and Imagination*, he presents several sermons in which the point of entry into our human reality

is a poem, a novel, a drama, or a film. One entitled "Easy
Rider" uses the two chief figures in the film of that name as
symbols of the rootlessness and alienation characteristic of
our age. Billy and the Captain are:

> Invulnerable (and therefore terribly vulnerable),
>    inarticulate,
>       and even disloyal to their own values,
> they move from place to place, never finding a place where
> they can open themselves, speak about their lives, and give
> themselves to other people. . . .
>    The movie raises a clear question, theirs and ours: How
> do we overcome alienation?
>    How do we find our way back . . . to ourselves and our
> fellow man, to those *interior* landscapes of peace.[22]

These are indeed *our* questions.

3. *We will preach Law not as an end in itself but in order
to serve the proclamation of the Gospel.*

This strictly instrumental nature of the Law is clear in
Luther's familiar statement of its purpose: "to disclose the
sin . . . and drive us to Christ."[23] Whether as accusation or
description, the Law is never terminal in the Christian sermon. It is always God's "alien" Word uttered for the sake
of his "proper" Word—which is the Word of his gracious
affirmation of us in Jesus Christ. A sermon therefore which
stops short with an exposure of people's guilt or an analysis
of their human plight is not yet a *Christian* sermon. Such
a sermon is a torso. It serves only to deepen the despair of
those who listen or to weight more heavily the burden of
guilt they carry. No liberating Word of acceptance and hope
has been announced.

Recollection of this principle will have important consequences for our self-image as preachers. We will take no
secret delight in the judging and exposing Word we are com-
missioned to deliver. We will not see ourselves as prosecut-
ing attorneys whose sole objective is to drive through to a

verdict of "guilty" against our hearers. Rather, our role is more that of surgeons who know they must cut in order to heal, or of therapists who understand the necessity of leading clients to insight which holds simultaneously the prospect of pain and the promise of renewal. Indeed, our preaching of Law will communicate a quality of empathy by which our hearers will know instinctively that we participate in the hurts and guilts we must sometimes bring to the level of consciousness.

Helmut Thielicke, in a sermon based on the petition of the Lord's Prayer, "Deliver us from evil," sums up the way in which preachers will proclaim the Law, whether as "hammer of judgment" or as "mirror of existence":

> May [the church] be a comforting beacon, proclaiming to all men that at least in one place in this world of hate and revenge there is love, because, beyond all comprehension, the Son of God died for this world. And if it must preach judgment, if it must call down woe upon the people and interpret the fearful signs of the times, then may it never do so pharisaically, as one who had no share in the great guilt. But rather may it do so as a mother, whose own soul is pierced through by a sword; may it do so as did Jesus Christ himself, who uttered the cry of judgment over Jerusalem in a voice that was choked with tears.[24]

## NOTES

1. John Steinbeck, *Travels with Charley* (New York: Viking Press, 1962), p. 71.
2. Jonathan Edwards, *Puritan Sage: Collected Writings of Jonathan Edwards,* ed. Vergilius Ferm (New York: Library Publishers, 1953), pp. 365–378.
3. Ragnar Bring, *Commentary on Galatians* (Philadelphia: Fortress Press, 1961), p. 178.
4. Martin Luther, "Lectures on Galatians" (1535), *LW* 26:406.
5. Ibid., *LW* 27:13.
6. Ibid.
7. *LW* 26:403, 404.
8. *LW* 26:309–310.
9. *LW* 26:310.

10. *LW* 26:315. Luther writes: ". . . hunger is the best cook. As the earth thirsts for rain, so the Law makes the troubled heart thirst for Christ. To such hearts Christ tastes the sweetest; to them he is joy, comfort, and life. Only then are Christ and his work understood correctly" (*LW* 26:329).

11. Martin Luther, "Sermons on the Gospel of St. John," *LW* 22:370–373.

12. "The Apology of the Augsburg Confession," *The Book of Concord*, ed. and trans. Theodore G. Tappert (Philadelphia: Fortress Press, 1959), p. 112.

13. Paul Tillich, *Systematic Theology*, 3 vols. (Chicago: University of Chicago Press, 1951, 1957, 1963), 2:44.

14. Heinrich Ott, *Theology and Preaching* (Philadelphia: Westminster Press, 1965), p. 60.

15. Ibid., p. 61.

16. Gerhard Ebeling, *Word and Faith* (Philadelphia: Fortress Press, 1960), p. 281.

17. Paul Tillich, "Communicating the Christian Message: A Question to Christian Ministers and Teachers," in *Theology of Culture*, ed. Robert C. Kimball (New York: Oxford University Press, 1959), pp. 203–204 (italics by H.G.S.).

18. Tillich, *Systematic Theology*, 2:46.

19. Edmund A. Steimle, *Are You Looking for God?* (Philadelphia: Fortress Press, 1957), p. 81.

20. John Vannorsdall, "The Siren Song of Wisdom's Maids," in *Renewal in the Pulpit*, ed. Edmund A. Steimle (Philadelphia: Fortress Press, 1966), pp. 40–41.

21. H. A. Williams, *The True Wilderness* (Philadelphia: J. P. Lippincott Co., 1965), pp. 29–30.

22. Charles L. Rice, *Interpretation and Imagination: The Preacher and Contemporary Literature* (Philadelphia: Fortress Press, 1970), pp. 149, 148.

23. Martin Luther, *LW* 26:315.

24. Helmut Thielicke, *Our Heavenly Father: Sermons on the Lord's Prayer* (New York: Harper and Brothers, 1960), p. 145.

# -3-

# GOSPEL:
# THE GIFT OF FORGIVENESS

One of the most compelling scenes in Alan Paton's *Cry, the Beloved Country* is a worship service in the House of the Blind high in the South African hills. Msimangu, a young priest, is preaching to his sightless congregation. Pastor Kumálo, his heart shattered by the knowledge that his only son has murdered a white man, listens:

> The voice shook and beat and trembled, not as the voice of an old man shakes and beats and trembles, nor as a leaf shakes and beats and trembles, but as a deep bell when it is struck. For it was not only a voice of gold, but it was the voice of a man whose heart was golden, reading from a book of golden words. . . .
> I, the Lord, have called thee in righteousness and will hold thine hand and keep thee. . . .
> And the voice rose, and the Zulu tongue was lifted and transfigured and the man too was lifted, as is one who comes to something greater than any of us. . . .
> I hear you my brother, there is no word I do not hear.[1]

The miracle of preaching has occurred! The Gospel has been proclaimed and received!

But why is it, in the preparation of a sermon, that the articulation of the Gospel often seems the hardest part? Is it because in a fallen world images of sin and brokenness always seem closer at hand than images of grace? Is it

34

because we as preachers find some strange corner of our egos more satisfied by exposing darkness than by announcing light? Is it because we ourselves scarcely believe the astonishing news of our own liberation, and therefore feel too little compulsion to speak it to others?

Whatever the reasons, preaching which stops short with the proclamation of Law is bad news and not Good News. It merely adds to the "nausea of words" which afflicts us in our age of mass communication. The preacher who in any sermon never moves beyond accusation or description has said nothing distinctive. In fact, there are probably many social scientists, editorial writers, political analysts, and poets who could say it better. The sermon which functions only as a mirror or as a hammer is abortive. It fails to reach its essential fruition in the Word which opens before us a way beyond our guilt and alienation.

We have already noted how in Ott's theological analysis of preaching the description of the reality of human "sin and wretchedness" is to be held in juxtaposition to the proclamation of what God has done to deliver us from our bondage. Likewise, Haselden insists that "the good sermon always presents the promise against the peril."[2] This is consistent with Luther's insistence that we preach God's "strange Word," the Law, only to prepare people to hear his "proper Word," the Gospel.[3] In short, Christian preaching is not primarily God's "No" spoken over against human existence but his "Yes."

In the previous chapter, we noted two modes by which Law can be preached. Now, as we turn to the consideration of the preaching of Gospel, it is important to state in a preliminary way a basic principle: the mode in which we have preached Law must find its correlate in the mode in which we proclaim the Gospel. If in a particular sermon the Law has been preached primarily as hammer of judgment, then the Gospel as forgiveness is its proper correlate. If, however, the Law as mirror of existence has exposed some aspect of our condition other than guilt, then a note of the Gospel appropriate to that aspect ought to be sounded in response. The meaning of this proposition will become more clear in the sections that follow.

## THE GOSPEL AS FORGIVENESS

The proclamation of the Gospel as forgiveness is in direct continuity with the Reformation heritage with its central doctrine of "justification by faith." To all who struggle with a burden of guilt impossible either to carry or to lay down, there comes the announcement that God in Christ has taken the burden upon himself. No longer need we exhaust ourselves in the futile effort to justify our own lives. Indeed, it is a sign of unbelief to do so, for God has promised to take that hopeless task off our hands and into his own.

This is the sermon Luther preached nearly every time he entered the pulpit. His sermons are endless variations on a theme, transposed in key according to text of season, and the theme is the Gospel. The Gospel is God revealing himself as merciful Father rather than angry Judge. The Gospel is God declaring sinners righteous, releasing us from our bondage to the Law into "the glorious liberty of the children of God," raising us who were "dead in trespasses and sins" into newness of life. Its true note sounds in a verse from Matthew, which Luther loved to quote: "Come to me, all who labor and are heavy laden, and I will give you rest" (Matt. 11:28).

At the center of this Gospel stands the man Jesus Christ. We need not "clamber into heaven" to find a gracious God, for in this man God has condescended to us. The lowly form of the Incarnation is designed especially for our comfort:

> . . . you must run directly to the manger and the mother's womb, embrace this Infant and Virgin's child in your arms, and look at him . . . born, being nursed, growing up, going about in human society, teaching, dying, rising again, ascending above all heavens, and having authority over all things. In this way you can shake off all terrors and errors, as the sun dispels the clouds.[4]

But this Word of the Gospel means nothing to us so long as we hear it as if at a distance. We must listen to it as though it were addressed to each of us personally. Luther stresses this in his exposition of Galatians 2:20b: "And the life I now live in the flesh I live by faith in the Son of God, who loved me and gave himself for me." "Who is this 'me'?" Luther asks, and he replies, "It is I."[5] It is one thing to believe that Christ gave himself for Peter, Paul, and the saints. It is quite another matter—but the crucial matter— to believe that he gave himself for *me*. Here, as Luther sees it, lies the central function of preaching: to help people appropriate to themselves all that God offers them in Christ.

> . . . Christ [ought] to be preached to the end that faith in him may be established that he may not only be Christ, but be Christ for you and me, and that what is said of him and is denoted in his name may be effectual in us. Such faith is produced and preserved in us by preaching why Christ came, what he brought and bestowed, what benefit it is to us to accept him.[6]

### PREACHING FORGIVENESS TODAY

Though we may agree with Luther, we know also that no formula or blueprint can guarantee that this "golden bell" of the Gospel will resound in our preaching. A sermon is a living organism, not a mechanical construct. For us, as for Luther, it grows out of a mysterious interchange among three living partners: the Word, the preacher, and the people. No rules determine its development and life. In the end, a sermon in which the Word of the Gospel is spoken and heard is a miracle and cannot be manipulated. Yet reference to certain principles may help us not to impede the dynamic process out of which proclamation is finally born. I will state four which seem to me to be important when we proclaim the Gospel as forgiveness in coordination with preaching of Law as judgment.

1. *We will search for an idiom which is intelligible to people today.*

Finding language which will communicate with reality and power is a key problem in the whole range of the homiletical task. The problem is particularly acute, however, in the proclamation of the Gospel as forgiveness. Here we are under special temptation to lapse into a vocabulary which, while of honored lineage, has been drained of much of its meaning for people today. Probably because the motifs of sin and forgiveness lie so close to the heart of the Christian message, phrases hallowed by long usage in piety and dogma have tended to cluster here with peculiar concentration. We have at hand, preserved in the tradition, as in amber, an instant vocabulary, a familiar "language of Canaan." It includes words like *atonement, redemption, propitiation,* and *justification.*

The difficulty with such words is that they are all rooted in spheres of life now foreign to our everyday experience— *propitiation* and *atonement* in the cult of animal sacrifice, *redemption* in the slave trade, *justification* in the Roman legal system. Such words no longer have the same living context for our people, so that a passage like the following is apt to be for them "inauthentic speech": "He paid the price for all your mistakes. He atoned, as the Bible puts it, for your sins. People like you and me are justified, put right with God, freely by his grace in Jesus Christ, whom God sent forth to be a substitutionary sacrifice for our sins."[7]

If we choose to use an array of images such as these to convey the reality of grace, we place ourselves and our listeners under an extraordinary handicap. Either we must work overtime—utilizing valuable minutes of the sermon—to provide a context of explanation in which the "meaning gap" can be reduced, or we will fall under the judgment which Ebeling states sharply: "Kerygma which is unintelligible conceals the true scandal and causes offense in the wrong way. As such it fails to call men to decision."[8]

One option open to us when we preach the Gospel as forgiveness is to search for idioms and images which grow out of the matrix of today's world. This is what Tillich did in his familiar translation of the Reformation doctrine of "justification by faith" into the formulation "to accept oneself as accepted in spite of being unacceptable."[9] The Gospel is the promise that God accepts us even though we are unacceptable, and faith is accepting the fact that this is so. Tillich drew his vocabulary from the field of depth psychology: his analogy was the relationship between therapist and patient. In a psychologically oriented age, this may suggest one set of helpful images. Notice how Tillich's formula is given homiletical expression in this passage from a Steimle sermon:

> That is what forgiveness, in its simplest terms, means: acceptance. Not because of your brains, your wit, or your good looks, not for the figure you cut on campus or in a career, not because you are "good," certainly, or even because you may be "better" than somebody else, but simply because you are you, irreplaceable, infinitely worthwhile in the eyes of God.
>
> The simplest and, I suppose, still the best analogy is the young child who is blessed with wise and loving parents; the child who, regardless of whether he is dull witted or bright, homely or handsome, devilish or well behaved, knows that he is accepted, loved, and constantly forgiven by his parents. And it is that child who, with an assurance he does not consciously recognize, bounds out of the house to play in the sun or hops off to school in the rain, not even aware that the reason why his life has daily joy and purpose and direction is just because he is accepted, forgiven, and loved.
>
> This is the assurance . . . the cross bestows upon those who linger in its shadow. For here we know it doesn't come easily. It costs. It costs suffering and rejection and death before we will kneel down and accept . . . the fact that we are accepted just as we are.[10]

Here the idiom is warm, human, analogic, and parabolic in contrast to the abstract dogmatic language of the passage quoted above. The preacher has struggled with the task which has always exercised those called to proclaim the Gospel—to find a profane (literally "in front of the temple") vocabulary in which to cast the message of grace. He has understood that an idiom which merely repeats the language of an earlier era may impede the Gospel rather than release it.

2. *We will take time to interpret the dynamics of forgiveness,
and not just announce it.*

The problem of communicating the Gospel of forgiveness
is deeper than simply selecting a contemporary vocabulary.
A way must be found to break open for people the actual
dynamics of the experience of forgiveness and to lead them
into its reality.

Here is a point in the preaching task where the roles of
preacher and teacher come into creative tension. As preacher,
herald, *kerux*, we simply proclaim the Gospel—announcing
its promise in the most direct way possible. As teacher we
are also called to interpret the Gospel—to unfold with care
and imagination its meaning and implications.

If in our preaching we content ourselves with merely announcing "God forgives you" or "Jesus died for your sins"
we are presupposing a situation which for many of our listeners may not in fact exist. We are presupposing that they are
able to flesh out such skeletal statements with a body of
meaning. In actuality a phrase like "Jesus died for your
sins" is theological shorthand which many listeners will be
utterly unable to translate. They are left with only the most
conventional and superficial notion as to how an execution
far back in history is related to the actual guilt which gnaws
at their hearts today. Likewise in their own daily relationships they may experience so little that can be characterized
as grace that the reality packed into a phrase like "God
forgives" will elude them.

No small part of the incomparable power of Jesus' preaching was his grasp of the fact that his listeners needed to be
led into the reality of the Good News he was announcing.
Parables like the Prodigal Son and the Laborers in the Vine-
yard are surely efforts to unfold, not simply to herald, the
dynamics of grace. His listeners were invited to identify
with the son or with the workers and to move with them
through a vicarious experience of the incredible nature of
undeserved and unexpected grace.

Notice how in the following two sermon excerpts the preacher assumes the role of interpreter as well as proclaimer. In the first, he is eager to disabuse his listeners of a false understanding of forgiveness so that they can enter into its true reality:

> Because so much is at stake here for all of us, we should be clear as to what forgiveness is. There is a widespread and really childish idea that what it means is being "let off," a complete acquittal, the overlooking of everything that was amiss. This would be immoral. It would not only be weak indulgence but a condoning of wrong. . . .
>
> Forgiveness is not the wiping out of all the consequences of sin; it is the restoration of a relationship. If I have wronged a friend and I go to him and ask him to forgive me, am I thinking only that I will get off scot free for the harm done? Surely not. Surely the idea of being "let off" does not touch the core of the matter. What I am really asking is that we should be to each other what we were before the offense was committed—the barrier between us taken away, the old confidence restored, the relationship of intimacy and trust renewed.
>
> And, says Christ, his death on the cross, confirming and climaxing all he taught, this is exactly what God is willing and eager to have happen between us and Himself—every barrier broken down, the personal filial relationship re-stored.[11]

Note how the preacher uses an analogy from our ordinary human relationships to communicate the nature of forgiveness. The appropriateness of this lies in the fact that forgiveness *is* a relationship and not a dogma. Its meaning, therefore, can best be expressed through a "story" in which people can be seen to interact in a way that is qualified by grace. This is the genius of Jesus' parables. The extraordinary way in which God deals with us is reflected in episodes out of ordinary life, notable only for the surprising initiative of radical love. This search for some human "parable of grace" is evident also in this passage from another sermon:

> I once knew a young man who was struggling with a very serious problem; he carefully tried to conceal the struggle from his best friend, because he was afraid that if the friend

found out, their friendship would be ruined. But at last the young man could stand it no longer, so he went to his friend and told him the whole story. And the friend replied: "I've known about it all along, and I've liked you in spite of it. . . ."

So it is in our relationship with God. After all, God has known about human sinfulness for a long time now. And if he loves us, it is not because we have succeeded in fooling him. If he loves us, he loves us in spite of everything. And when our distrust and hardness of heart break down enough so that we can face the worst about ourselves, what we find in his presence is not rejection, but acceptance.[12]

3. *We will address people with the promise of forgiveness as personally and directly as possible.*

The Gospel is not for people "in general" or for human-kind in the abstract. It is for actual persons all with names and histories uniquely their own. The Word in preaching is to be addressed to the congregation in such a way that every listener will know it is intermingled with his or her particular history. The great Story will overlay each smaller story. Each listener will be moved, as was Kumálo, to say: "I hear you my brother. There is no word I do not hear."

We have already encountered this intensely personal dimension of the Gospel's meaning in Luther's commentary on Galatians 2:20b: "Who is this 'me'? It is I." Luther states this theme still more boldly in a Christmas Day sermon preached in 1530:

So great should that light which declares that he is my Savior become in my eyes that I can say: Mary, you did not bear this child for yourself alone, . . . but for me, . . . even though you held him in your arms and wrapped him in swaddling clothes. . . . This child . . . is not only his mother's son. I have more than the mother's estate; he is more mine than Mary's, for he was born for me, for the angel said, "To you" is born the Savior. Then ought you to say, Amen, I thank thee, dear Lord.[13]

H. H. Farmer many years ago pointed out the critical importance of pronouns for establishing the tone of the sermon.[14] The generic words *man* or *mankind* are coldly abstract, only slightly improved upon by the third person *he, she,* or *they.* These are words of indirect address which allow a listener to hold the message they convey at a distance. *He* or *they* are always someone else. The first person plurals *we* and *our* are more inclusive. They are uniting words, comprehending speaker and listener under the same arc. But it is only with the second person pronoun *you* that we move into a direct, personal mode of address. We are properly cautious in utilizing this form in passages of heavy judgment, but in addressing people with the promise of the Gospel it is often an entirely natural form. In the passage just quoted Luther instinctively slips into it in the final sentence though the prior material had been in the form of a first person soliloquy.

Here is a passage from a contemporary sermon in which the second person style of direct address is used with great force: "If you are one of those wandering around out there like sheep without a shepherd, you should know that Christ is for you. He has a heart for you. He died for you. He knows all about you. He calls to you."[15] If you alter that passage by substituting forms of the general *man*, the third person *they,* or even the first person *we*, the change in tone is dramatically toward the abstract and impersonal. A sermon cast consistently in such style takes on the "to whom it may concern" tone of a mimeographed form letter. But preaching in which the listener is addressed directly with the promise of forgiveness communicates the "I-Thou" quality which is the essence of living encounter. Such preaching literally gets personal. When this happens, words have the possibility of becoming event, a happening for the listener.

4. *We will preach forgiveness with a clear focus on the person and work of Jesus.*

Placed alongside the point we have just made, this statement means that our preaching of forgiveness will be bifocal.

It will hold in view both actual persons in our congregation who need the Word of grace and Jesus who is its mediator. The preacher becomes the third party who opens up between these two a living interchange. This fact is what makes preaching in a profound sense a priestly office. Paul speaks of his preaching to the Gentiles as his "priestly service of the Gospel of God" (Rom. 15:16). The preacher is the intermediary between Jesus, *the* mediator, and his body, the church.

This guideline does not imply that the christological content of a sermon can be measured by counting the number of times the name of Jesus is mentioned. It is possible to preach Christ legalistically and mechanistically. He can be presented as the embodiment of an ethical ideal which people must attain or as a factor in a doctrine they are obligated to believe. On the other hand, it is possible to preach God's forgiveness of the guilty without reference to Jesus. Otherwise we would have to rule out such passages as Hosea 11: 1–11 or Isaiah 53 as proclamations of grace.

Yet granting what we have just said, in preaching forgiveness we will not be so reticent about "naming the Name" that we blur what is central and distinctive in the message we are called to proclaim. The person and work of Jesus *do* stand at the center of the Gospel. The unique revelation of God's forgiving grace in Jesus' life, death, and resurrection does not negate what God manifests of himself elsewhere but gathers it to such a point of brilliance that all the rest is illumined. Not to point to Jesus when trying to communicate God's grace to the guilty is to bypass what remains for our world the clearest image of utterly self-giving Love. Jesus is supremely God's parable to us.

This is why the Gospels themselves have always provided the central texts in the history of the church's preaching. It is why we as preachers are instinctively drawn to pericopes in which the man Jesus is shown in living interaction with people in their need—the leper, the paralytic, blind Bartimaeus, or Peter in the instabilities of his discipleship. Here we see the movements of the immeasurable grace of God reduced to human scale. We can identify with these persons to whom "the man for others" offered himself. Each such episode becomes a little Gospel in which the great Gospel is enacted. Jesus is held before us as the paradigm of God's own gracious action towards us—an action which reaches its fullest and final expression at the cross and the tomb.

Excerpts from an Easter sermon by Karl Barth preached to prisoners in the Basel jail are notable for their clear christological focus and also for their expression of the purpose of all preaching from the events related in the Gospels:

> The most terrible thing possible had taken place: the other side had won. Jesus was definitely no longer there. And they themselves? How often had they misunderstood him, and thought and lived quite differently from the way he had told them. . . . Repentance, mourning, fear was all that was left them: a heap of broken fragments . . .
>
> To them came the risen Jesus and stepped into their midst. Why? To make himself, in the might of God's great mercy, the head of this forlorn group, of these miserable and burdened, gloomy and frightened and cowardly men—the head of this thoroughly sick body. He did that in the simplest way imaginable: "Peace be with you," he said to them. . . .
>
> Dear friends, we were not there when the risen Jesus . . . came into their midst. We cannot see him now as directly as they could . . . But in our way, indirectly, that is in the mirror of the narrative and so of the witness, the confession, the proclamation of the first community, we too can and may see him here and now.[16]

## NOTES

1. Alan Paton, *Cry, the Beloved Country* (New York: Charles Scribner's Sons, 1948), pp. 89–90.

2. Haselden, *The Urgency of Preaching*, p. 55.

3. Luther warns that preachers who are so occupied with the Law that they neglect the Gospel are guilty of "wounding and not binding up, smiting and not healing, killing and not making alive, leading down into hell and not bringing back again,

humbling and not exalting" ("The Freedom of a Christian" [1520], *LW* 31:364).

5. *LW* 26:176.

6. *LW* 31:357.

7. From a radio sermon.

8. Gerhard Ebeling, *Theology and Proclamation* (Philadelphia: Fortress Press, 1966), p. 39.

9. Paul Tillich, *The Courage to Be* (New Haven: Yale University Press, 1962), p. 164.

10. Edmund A. Steimle, *Are You Looking for God?* (Philadelphia: Fortress Press, 1957), pp. 37–38.

11. Robert J. McCracken, "Forgiveness—Human and Divine," an unpublished sermon.

12. David E. Roberts, *The Grandeur and Misery of Man* (New York: Oxford University Press, 1955), pp. 55–56.

13. Martin Luther, "Sermon on the Afternoon of Christmas Day" (1530), *LW* 51:214–215.

14. See H. H. Farmer, *The Servant of the Word* (Philadelphia: Fortress Press, 1964 [original edition 1941]), pp. 43–44.

15. Oswald Hoffman, *A Tough Profession* (St. Louis: Lutheran Laymen's League, 1968), p. 5.

16. Karl Barth, *Call for God* (New York: Harper & Row, 1967), pp. 120, 121, 124.

# -4-

# GOSPEL:
# ANTIPHON TO EXISTENCE

In Chapter 2 we discussed two modes of preaching Law. The first we characterized as "hammer of judgment." Here the Word of God confronts us as our accuser. When the Law is preached in this mode it is obvious that the Gospel proclaimed as forgiveness, or justification, is its proper correlate. In each case the focus is on the conscience—first to stir it out of complacency into guilt, and then to lead it to a place of security in grace.

The situation is more complex when we turn to the preaching of Law as "mirror of existence." Here, as we noted, the Law functions not as an accusatory Word from beyond us but as a threat which rises from within the actualities of life. Our goal in preaching is not so much to stir the conscience as to awaken consciousness. Listeners are to be helped to a recognition of the reality of their life in this world, a reality of which terms like *alienation, anxiety*, and *despair* are descriptive.

Here lies the difficulty for our preaching. Whereas the Gospel as forgiveness is a natural and obvious correlate for the Law as judgment, there is no such single pair of co-ordinates for the Law preached as "mirror of existence." Any analysis of our human condition which moves beyond the category of guilt must include many terms. We have already employed such words as *alienation, doubt, despair, meaning-*

47

*lessness, emptiness, brokenness,* and *transiency.* To answer only to these a whole spectrum of positive words would be needed—*unification, trust, hope, meaning, fullness, healing,* and *enduringness.* Thus no single word or phrase can characterize the Gospel when it is preached in answer to the Law as "mirror of existence."

## THE GOSPEL AS ANTIPHON

In this chapter we will try to comprehend the variety just noted by speaking in general terms of the Gospel as "antiphon to existence." The word *antiphon* has a long liturgical tradition in the church, but our concern will be more with its literal meaning, rooted in the two Greek words *anti* (in return) and *phonos* (sounding). An antiphon is a voice lifted in response to another voice. It is not a mere echo. It speaks with a content independent of, yet related to, the voice it answers. For example, in the office of Matins the congregation's response, "And my mouth shall show forth thy praise," is related antiphonally to the liturgist's petition, "O Lord, open thou my lips."

In terms of the preaching task, to speak of the Gospel as "antiphon to existence" is to suggest that the actual content of its address will be qualified but not determined by the specific aspect of the human condition which the Law as "mirror" has reflected. In order to see how this antiphonal movement actually occurs we will look at ways in which the Gospel has actually been formulated and preached by certain contemporary interpreters of the Christian faith in response to selected aspects of existence. Before that, however, it is important to state three preliminary considerations.

First, it must be kept in mind that just as the Law as "judgment" and the Law as "description" are related, so are the Gospel as "forgiveness" and the Gospel as "antiphon." Judgment and forgiveness are fully as antiphonal in character as, for example, despair and hope. Furthermore, guilt may be a major element in the structure of despair, so that forgiveness will be a clear note in the articulation of the Gospel as hope. The purpose of the twofold schema we are employing is not to separate sharply realities which in actuality exist together. It is rather, for the sake of analysis, to distinguish between a mode of preaching Law and Gospel which has judgment and forgiveness as its dominant themes and a mode in which the primary stress is upon aspects of the human condition other than guilt and upon elements in the Gospel other than forgiveness. Outside such analysis—in actual sermons and certainly in life itself—the realities of judgment and forgiveness interplay with others we have noted and are themselves antiphonal in character.

Second, we should note that categories other than judgment and forgiveness had their place in earlier periods of Christian proclamation. Luther, for instance, knew about anxiety, despair, and the fear of death as well as about guilt. This is apparent in his famous *Anfechtungen*—bouts of spiritual anguish compounded of "all the doubt, turmoil, pang, tremor, panic, despair, desolation, and deprivation which invade the spirit of man."[1] It is arguable that the experience of guilt lies at the vortex of these swirling elements, yet it is also true that Luther can speak of the human condition in terms other than guilt.[2] Correspondingly, he can declare the power of the Gospel to assuage our hearts not only in matters of sin but "in all other troubles."[3] What we are doing, therefore, is to lift into a more prominent position a mode of proclaiming the Gospel which in earlier eras had a subordinate place.

Third, the imprecise, overlapping character of the correlates we will use in our illustrations of the Gospel as "antiphon to existence" should be kept in mind. Those to which attention will be given are: alienation and reconciliation, anxiety and certitude, despair and hope, transiency and homecoming. There is only relative precision in these and other possible pairings. Healing, for example, could be substituted for reconciliation, or doubt for anxiety. Furthermore, these and other sets do not exist in isolation from each other. A sense of alienation, for instance, is an ingredient in the mood of despair, even as the experience of certitude contributes to healing or reconciliation. We are dealing with a complex nexus of realities, separable only for purposes of analysis.

## REFLECTIONS AND ANTIPHONS

With the above considerations in mind, we will now turn to four sets of coordinates. On the one hand, we will describe reflections of our human condition which the Law as mirror holds before us. Over against these reflections, we will set antiphonal phrasings of the Gospel as these have found expression in contemporary theology and preaching.

### Alienation and Reconciliation

The word *alienation* points to the fractured condition of the self and of the world which environs the self. We experience ourselves as unwhole within, and we are as often aware of our separation from as of our relatedness with reality outside ourselves. Furthermore, the communities in which we live are fragmented and polarized. A contemporary artist has portrayed a scene which shows a group of people staring in every direction—except at each other. Man in history is *homo incommunicado*—man out of communication. Each of us, in the words of Tillich, is "estranged from the ground of being, from other beings, and from himself."[4]

It is also Tillich who suggests a phrasing of the Gospel which brings it into antiphonal relation with life seen under the rubric of estrangement or alienation. He notes the root of the word *salvation* in the Greek *salvus* (healed). Thus what the Gospel proclaims is the meaning of a "healing reality"[5] with the power of "reuniting what is estranged, giving a center to what is split, overcoming the split between God and man, man and his world, man and himself."[6] This "healing reality" is operative in all times and places but is centered fully in the One who embodies the "New Being," Jesus as the Christ. As we encounter Jesus and are drawn into the reality of the "New Being" we begin to experience integration and reconciliation at all levels of our estrangement. Under the conditions of life in history, however, this unification never reaches completion. Just as the Gospel offers forgiveness "in spite of" the continued presence of sin, so the "healing reality" of the Gospel is present "in the midst of" all the disintegrative forces which continue to destroy our wholeness. Total and universal healing in the self and in society is an eschatological reality waiting "beyond history."[7]

The late David Roberts preached a sermon entitled "Man's Isolation and God's Intervention" in which the antiphonal themes of alienation and reconciliation are brought together in a creative way. In the early part of the sermon he explores the sense of isolation and loneliness which afflicts us all in the modern world, producing "a sort of practical atheism which everyone of us carries around in his heart." Because we cannot stand isolation we seek desperate solutions by lashing out at the world in lust or greed, or by submerging ourselves in various collectives. The Christian Gospel offers another alternative:

> The Christian Gospel speaks directly to that isolated man who dwells within the heart of every one of us. For its message is this: that although solitude may be the last word so far as we are concerned, it is not the last word so far as God is concerned. Although we may shut ourselves off from God, God will not leave us alone. Man has to come to terms with his Creator, either through the agony of estrangement or through faith in Christ's reconciling love; but twist and turn as he may, man cannot really escape into isolation.
>
>> Whither shall I go from thy Spirit?
>> Or wither shall I flee from thy presence?
>> If I ascend up into heaven, Thou art there;
>> If I make my bed in Sheol, behold, Thou art there.
>> If I take the wings of the morning
>> And dwell in the uttermost parts of the sea;
>> Even there shall thy hand lead me,
>> And thy right hand shall hold me.
>
> This is our faith and confidence; this is the sense of companionship which girds us when all trust in men has be-

trayed us; this is our hope of fellowship while fellowship
is being destroyed on every side. . . . beyond the guilt we
cannot escape, beyond the sin and ignorance that hem us
in, we are called into the fellowship of One who understands us all along. No matter what suffering or sorrow may
lie ahead, he has been there before us, and he waits for us
at the end.[8]

## Anxiety and Certitude

Anxiety is a comprehensive reality which embraces other
elements in the structure of our existence. Unlike fear,
which is related to a specific object, anxiety is diffuse. It is
characterized by a pervasive "free-floating" quality.[9] Gerhard Ebeling appears to be describing anxiety when he speaks
of the "radical questionableness" under which we live.[10]
This questionableness pertains not only to the fact that we
must render an accounting for our lives but, more broadly,
to "the unintelligibility of reality as a whole" of which the
supreme symbol is the idea of *deus absconditus*, "the absent
God."[11]

In this threatened situation, where nothing coheres and
God seems absent, the Gospel reaches us as a Word which
brings us certitude.[12] It does not extricate us from our
anxiety-producing situation, but as Ebeling describes it:

Faith gives certainty to existence. . . . The certainty of faith
. . . is taking sure steps, although no road is visible, hoping
although there is nothing to look for, refusing to despair
although things are desperate, having ground under us although we step into a bottomless pit.[13]

The source of such certitude is Jesus, who in his own life
and death bore witness to the power of faith to overcome all
threats. He is the One who took upon himself all the nega-
tivities of human life and by faith overcame them. Thus he
opens to us the possibility of living in the midst of the total
questionableness of existence with a certitude that we have
a standing ground on something "ultimately valid and reli-
able."[14] We receive from him, in Tillich's terms, "the courage to be" even while tragic and destructive forces assault us.

A Christmas Eve sermon by Karl Barth illustrates the proclamation of the Gospel as certitude, spoken antiphonally to the Law as anxiety. His text is John 16:33: "In the world you face anxiety; but take heart, I have overcome the world." Early in the sermon Barth engages in an extensive dissection of the anatomy of anxiety. This is done with concreteness and specificity so that listeners of all sorts will have a chance of catching their reflection in the mirror he holds up. Ultimately, beneath all our other anxieties, Barth sees "the great anxiety . . . that we shall find our life surrounded by death, by utter extinction looming upon all sides, and by the nothingness to which life is subjected without hope of being saved."[15]

The springboard for his proclamation of the Gospel in the face of our threatened existence is the phrase of the text: ". . . but take heart."

"Take heart" does not mean: Just think of something else. Jump across the thing that is causing your anxiety. Run away from your anxiety . . . Take heart means: open your eyes and look up: to the hills from whence comes your aid —and look forward: to the few paces you can take now without hindrance . . .

Yes, but can we do this? . . . The answer is: Certainly *nobody on his own resources* . . . Everybody without exception can, however, take heart if he listens to the word telling him that he can and must take heart, when it is spoken to him by the one who himself, as true son of God and son of man, came into the world in which we face anxiety. In the midst of it all, he himself felt the greatest anxiety—"My God, my God, why have you abandoned me?"—but he has conquered this world, reconciled it with God, and so set a limit to the anxiety which we experience. From this limit, set by him, there shines forth to us, the people that walk in darkness, a great light. By seeing this light, following this light—by looking toward him who makes it shine upon us, by holding fast to him, by believing in him as we say— we have this word that we shall be free to take heart: free to be set at rest, not before the storm, nor after the storm, but right in the middle of the storm of our anxiety, when we are in direst distress and do *not* know where to turn.[16]

*Despair and Hope*

Despair is anxiety translated into the future tense. To face the future without hope is to exist in despair. Despair sees existence locked irretrievably within the realities which the past has built into the present. There appears to be "no exit" from such a situation. To live in despair is to conclude that present reality represents the termination of every prospect, the closure of all possibility, the exhaustion of all potentiality. Jürgen Moltmann has called despair "the rigidifying and freezing of the truly human element, which hope alone can keep flowing and free."[17] Those who despair believe themselves literally to have reached a dead end. Thus despair is a "little death" and finds in actual death its final symbol.

Moltmann can be taken as representative of a tendency in contemporary theology to articulate the Gospel, over against despair, in terms of hope. Basic to his formulation is his distinction between "epiphany religions and faith in terms of promise."[18] In an epiphany religion the deity makes a complete disclosure of himself, and the worshipper participates in his eternal being by performing sacred rites at a shrine hallowed by the epiphany. In biblical religion, however, the stress is not so much on God's self-manifestation as on the Word of promise spoken in a revelatory event. The present becomes neither an occasion for despair nor a moment of utopian fulfillment in mystical or cultic union. The present is rather the moment in which God speaks a Word of promise which allows us to make a "break-away toward the future."[19] We meet this God of promise in the history of Israel and especially in Jesus, whose ministry, death, and resurrection constitute an "event of promise." Particularly in the resurrection we encounter a "new possibility" for ourselves and for our world. Hope is awakened to "see reality and mankind in the hand of him whose voice calls into history from its end, 'Behold, I make all things new.' ..."[20]

Yet hope is not to be confused with fulfillment. The reality of the kingdom is always hidden in this life beneath all that contradicts it. But those who have heard the Word of promise are enabled "to bear 'the cross of the present' " and to "hold to what is dead, and hope for the unexpected."[21] Thus the Gospel as hope becomes for us the antiphon of despair. It liberates us from the prison of the past and the present into a future whose only horizon is God's promise of "a new heaven and a new earth in which righteousness dwells."

Advent, of course, is one season when this note of hope should ring with special clarity in our preaching. The eschatological visions in the Advent lessons are not to be taken literally, but they affirm that each of our biographies and our human story as a whole do not run into dead ends. They counter our personal defeats and our despair over the course of history with the promise that nothing in us or in our world will have the last word. The eschatological theme proclaimed in Advent declares that to God belongs the last word. We know this because in Jesus Christ he has spoken the "middle word," the Word on which everything turns as on a hinge.

It is at Easter, however, that we both listen for and preach the most powerful Word of hope. D. T. Niles has called Easter "the signature of life" which God has written across history, countermanding "the signature of death."[22] In an Easter sermon once preached by James Stewart this Word of hope forms a repeated antiphon to our bleak despair:

> . . . many in these tumultuous days are trembling for the ark of God, haunted by the fear that the powers of darkness may ultimately defeat the dreams for which Christ died. Many are paralyzed by that terrible doubt. But Easter means that God has already taken the measure of the evil forces at their worst and most malignant, that He has met the challenge precisely at that point and routed the darkness and settled the issue. Rejoice that the Lord is arisen!
>   Or the trouble may be more personal. Many are feeling strained and depressed and tired out, and quite inadequate

for life, worried by the failure and muddle of their own experience. But Easter means a living, radiant Christ walking at your side on the weariest Emmaus road. Rejoice that the Lord is arisen!

Or the burden of the mystery may be heavier still. It may be that someone whom you loved the best has passed out of sight forever across the river, journeying away to the country from whose bourne no traveller returns. But Easter means One has returned, to tell you of the glory yonder. Rejoice that the Lord is arisen![23]

## Transiency and Homecoming

Transiency refers to our sense of tentativeness with respect to life. It is the recognition, often only partly conscious, that "all flesh is grass," and that impermanency and decay are the marks of the whole creation. Nothing, from the bloom of a rose to the deepest of our human relationships, can be counted upon to endure. Everything is subject to flux, change, and finally dissolution.

There are many forces in modern life which heighten our sense of temporariness. Technological and social change disrupt established patterns of life and remove familiar landmarks. Geographical mobility has turned us into "a nation of strangers" and deepened our sense of rootlessness. It has become literally true for many in our generation that "here we have no continuing city."

The conclusive mark of our transiency is death. Death tears away the last veil of illusion we may harbor about the lastingness of our place in this world. No rampart of achievement, security, or intimacy we throw up around ourselves can fend off this "last enemy" who will breach the wall and violate the inner citadel of the self.

In antiphonal response to the fact of our transiency, the Gospel addresses us with a Word about a Reality which endures at the center and to which we are invited to return, as children to their true and lasting home. It proclaims to us that though "the grass withers and the flower fades . . . , the Word of our God will stand forever" (Isa. 40:8). Underlying all the flux and decay within us and around us there is a gracious, beckoning power which time cannot ravage. The ultimate sign of this reality is given to us in the cross and resurrection of Jesus. Here the eternal Word made itself vulnerable to our transiency and subject to death itself. But "death had no dominion," and the Easter event speaks to us, even in the midst of the inescapable tentativeness of our existence, of the ultimate invulnerability and accessibility of love.

These antiphonal themes reach expression in a sermon by Edmund Steimle on the text Hebrews 11:13–16, which includes the words, ". . . they were strangers and exiles on the earth." Our fundamental problem is that we resist this description of our situation. Our world, that was meant to be only an inn for transients, we try desperately and unsuccessfully to turn into a permanent home. The hordes of refugees in our modern world are tragic symbols of what in fact is the true situation of us all. We are "passing travellers."

Steimle voices the Gospel over against this description of our existence in terms of "homecoming." He offers not the abrogation of our transient status in this world but rather a shift in its position in our lives. Outside faith the sense of exile dominates the center, despite all our efforts to pretend that we are at home and secure. Faith consists of the acceptance of the fact that this world offers no ultimate resting place; indeed, faith removes the need for it, for it has already found a more fundamental citizenship and homeland in the love of God:

Only as we know that this earth is not our true home can we ever find ourselves truly at home here. And it is out of this apparent contradiction, this tension, that the life of the Christian grows and develops: no longer the aching home-sickness or the frantic efforts to transform the inn into a permanent residence. The estrangement and the exile are transferred from the center of life to the peripheral and passing. A man is at home in this lovely, fascinating, and often tragic world bec use he knows where his true home lies.[24]

But even with this paradoxical assurance in our hearts there is no escaping the final mark of our transiency—death. It stands at the end of our road as the nemesis of every ruse by which we have tried to cheat the inexorable erosion of time. This passage from a sermon by Paul Tillich places the power of love in juxtaposition to the claims of death:

> It is love, human and divine, which overcomes death in nations and generations and in all the horror of our time. Help has become almost impossible in the face of the monstrous powers we are experiencing. Death is given power over everything finite, especially in our period of history. But death is given no power over love. Love is stronger. It creates something new out of the destruction caused by death; it bears everything and overcomes everything. . . . It rescues each of us, for love is stronger than death.[25]

In still another sermon Tillich makes explicit the ground of our hope in the enduringness of love. It is because of Good Friday and Easter that

> . . . the earth not only ceases to be the solid ground of life; she also ceases to be the lasting cave of death. Resurrection is not something added to the death of him who is the Christ; but it is implied in his death. . . . No longer is the universe subject to the law of death out of birth. It is subjected to the higher law, to the law of life out of death by the death of him who represented eternal life.[26]

## GOSPEL IN THE MIDST OF EXISTENCE

In summary, the preaching of Law as "mirror of existence" requires the preaching of Gospel as "antiphon to existence." Just as in our preaching of Law we "mirror" certain negative aspects of our common humanity, so in our proclamation of the Gospel we are to respond antiphonally with appropriate affirmations. We have noted and illustrated four paired motifs: alienation and reconciliation, anxiety and certitude, despair and hope, transiency and homecoming. Others of course are possible, and it becomes our task when we preach to match articulations of Law as "mirror" and Gospel as "antiphon" as sensitively and precisely as we can.

It is also important for us to preserve—analogous to the "in spite of" character of the Gospel as forgiveness—the "in the midst of" character of the Gospel as "antiphon." We will avoid the false promise that the Gospel resolves the tensions or removes the contradictions of existence. We will rather help our hearers see how the Gospel makes healing, hope, or certitude possible even while their contraries are unabatedly present.

The following pastoral conversation between a German army chaplain in World War II and Hans, a young officer, illustrates this antiphonal quality of the Gospel which we will struggle to let resound in our preaching. At the time, the German army was moving toward certain defeat in the mountains of Yugoslavia. Hans was in the depths of abject despair. The world continued to turn on its course absolutely unmindful that his young life was about to be snuffed out in an instant by a bullet or wasted away by degrees in a prison camp. Did anyone take any notice at all?

"God knows it," I said.

"I cannot believe it. He is too great. He doesn't bother about individuals."

"Don't ask whether he does. Ask first of all what it would mean if he did."

"It would mean that besides me and my mother there was somebody who cared about me."

"What does that mean, 'cared about'?"

"Well, it means that he worried about me like my mother does now, but God does not need to worry, that is human language."

"Stick to the point, you must be clear about this. Why does your mother worry about you?"

"Because she loves me, because I matter to her."

"Hans, you blind man, that is the simplest and most beautiful definition of love that you gave so casually. If someone loves me then I matter to them. I am as important to them as they are to themselves, or as I am to myself."

"Yes, that is why one feels so desperate in our situation. You have the feeling that you are important to yourself and perhaps to your mother, or some other woman, but that is all, and to everyone else you do not matter in the least."

"That is the demarcation line between despair and meaningfulness. The love of God is the meaning of your life, and cannot be destroyed even in the Jugoslav concentration camp. It amounts to just this: I am as important to God as I am to myself, and as he is to himself. Draw a cross on your camp bed, and repeat that sentence three times whenever the love of God is mentioned. Then you will understand what the Gospel is, and the joy that overcomes the world."²⁷

## NOTES

1. Roland Bainton, *Here I Stand* (New York: Abingdon-Cokesbury Press, 1950), p. 42.

2. "Luther had experiences which he describes as attacks of despair *(Anfechtung)*, as the frightful threat of a complete meaninglessness. . . . Luther in these moments, and in the descriptions he gave of them, anticipated the descriptions of them by modern existentialism" (Paul Tillich, *The Courage to Be* [New Haven: Yale University Press, 1962], p. 70.

3. In a sermon on Matthew 11:28, Luther says: "He does not say with this or that difficulty, but simply says, 'all who are heavy laden.' . . . he not only refreshes us in the anxiety and assaults of sin, but he will be with us in all other troubles" ("Sermon on St. Matthias Day" [1525], *LW* 51:129–130).

4. Paul Tillich, *Systematic Theology,* 3 vols. (Chicago: University of Chicago Press, 1951, 1957, 1963), 1:46.

5. Ibid., 1:209.

6. Ibid., 2:166.

7. Ibid., 3:282.

8. David E. Roberts, *The Grandeur and Misery of Man* (New York: Oxford University Press, 1955), pp. 136, 142.

9. Tillich, *Courage to Be,* pp. 36–39.

10. Gerhard Ebeling, "Theology and the Evidentness of the Ethical," *Journal for Theology and Church* 2 (1965): 124.

11. Ibid.

12. I have deliberately used the word *certitude* instead of *certainty,* the word chosen by Ebeling's translator. "CERTAINTY may stress the existence of objective unquestionable proofs; CERTITUDE may stress a faith strong enough to resist all attacks" (*Webster's Seventh New Collegiate Dictionary* [Springfield, Mass.: G. & C. Merriam Company, 1965], p. 136, s.v. *certainty* and *certitude*).

13. Gerhard Ebeling, *Word and Faith* (Philadelphia: Fortress Press, 1960), p. 240.

14. Gerhard Ebeling, *The Nature of Faith* (Philadelphia: Fortress Press, 1961), p. 131.
15. Karl Barth, *Call for God* (New York: Harper & Row, 1967), p. 110.
16. Ibid., pp. 111–112.
17. Jürgen Moltmann, *Theology of Hope* (New York: Harper & Row, 1965), p. 22.
18. Ibid., p. 95.
19. Ibid., p. 150.
20. Ibid., p. 26.
21. Ibid., p. 31.
22. D. T. Niles, *Preaching the Gospel of the Resurrection* (Philadelphia: Westminster Press, 1953), p. 77.
23. James Stewart, *Twenty Centuries of Great Preaching*, ed. Clyde E. Fant, Jr. and William M. Pinson, Jr. (Waco, Texas: Word Books, 1971), 11:198–199.
24. Edmund A. Steimle, *Disturbed by Joy* (Philadelphia: Fortress Press, 1967), p. 128.
25. Paul Tillich, *The New Being* (New York: Charles Scribner's Sons, 1955), pp. 173–174.
26. Ibid., p. 178.
27. Helmut Gollwitzer, *Unwilling Journey* (Philadelphia: Fortress Press, 1953), pp. 42–43.

# -5-

# THE CALL TO
# OBEDIENCE

The German poet Heine is reputed to have said on his death bed, "God will forgive; that's his business." Whether fact or fiction, that cavalier remark illustrates a problem with which the church has had to contend from the beginning. The more radically the church proclaims the Gospel of a God who affirms and forgives fully and unconditionally, the more it risks the possibility that those who hear will respond without moral seriousness.

Already in the first century Paul had to face this distortion of his message. This is part of the burden of his letter to the church in Rome. Having spent the first five chapters laying out as clearly and forcibly as possible the meaning of the righteousness that is by faith, he anticipates a misunderstanding: "What shall we say then? Are we to continue in sin that grace may abound?" (Rom. 6:1). If God justifies precisely the ungodly, does it not follow that the more ungodly we are the more brilliantly God's unconditional grace will shine by contrast? At least if we are made righteous by God's act and not by our own works, there certainly is no need for us to bother ourselves with moral effort. God has seen to it all without that. Paul writes off such specious logic with two blunt sentences in which one can still feel his exasperation: "By no means! How can we who died to sin live in it?" (6:2). There follows then a powerful description of the meaning of baptism as dying to the old life of sin and rising to new life in Christ.

It is not surprising therefore that the Reformation, with its fresh proclamation of the Pauline "justification by faith," produced also new possibilities of misinterpreting that affirmation. There have always been those who have almost willfully perverted the gift of freedom from guilt into the license of freedom to sin.

It must also be admitted that we preachers have involuntarily aided and abetted this problem. In our nervousness not to introduce a falsifying note of "works righteousness" into the Gospel of free grace, we have tended to keep silent about the quality of life which issues from it. We have bypassed the issue of response or obedience to God's sovereign will. It is enough, we have assumed, to announce as clearly and persuasively as we can all that God has done for us in Christ and then leave to the Holy Spirit the whole question of Christian obedience.

## LUTHER AND "GOOD WORKS"

There are passages in Luther in which Christ is declared so emphatically to be "the end of the Law" that its function in the life of the Christian seems to have ceased. The Christian, living out of the vitality of faith, simply produces good works spontaneously. He has "no need of a teacher of good works, but he does whatever the occasion calls for, and all is well done."[1] His obedience to God is no longer external and constrained but is as natural a product of the indwelling Spirit as is the "good fruit" produced by a healthy tree. The Christian can no more fail to exhibit a good life than a rock lying in the sun can fail to grow warm. Luther also uses the analogy of the mutual service of a husband and wife in a happy marriage. They do for each other what is needful without any instruction: "Confidence alone teaches them all this, and even more than is necessary."[2] Such language, suggesting a virtual "automatism of works," seems to imply that to the Christian the Law need no longer be preached.

A closer reading of Luther, however, makes it clear that such a conclusion is unwarranted.[3] In the first place, the Christian, along with all others, is still subject to the Law in its "political use." As long as he is in this world, he cannot escape the orders of state, economy, family, and institutional church, and as a participant in them he is subject to the divine mandate which prescribes their rightful patterns. The secular responsibilities of those who are justified are never abrogated. In fact, because they know that the Author of the Law is also a loving and forgiving Father they fulfill their common duties with new joy and freedom.

Further, the Law has continuing significance for the Christian in its "theological use." This is so because the Christian is always at the same time justified and sinner. In opposition to the working of the Spirit, the flesh—"that powerful jackass"[4]—still pursues its ungodly course. Therefore the Christian, so long as he lives on earth, never ceases to have to do with the accusations of the Law. Because sin is always present the Christian life is "nothing else than a daily baptism, once begun and ever continued."[5] Each day there must be a drowning of the old Adam and a rising to life of the new man in Christ.

But the question remains whether there is a basis here for any positive word about the content of the life of this new man in Christ. Is there a legitimate place in our teaching and preaching for instruction as to the actual shape of the life that flowers from justification and for exhortation toward its fulfillment? Here the answer is unquestionably "Yes."

In his Galatians commentary, for example, Luther follows the powerful interpretation of "justification by faith," which has preoccupied him up to the point of 5:13, with an equally clear exposition of "the commandment to love" by which the Christian is bound.[6] This love is a reflexive love in that it acts out on earth the same pattern of love which has come down to us from heaven in Christ. We become, as it were, "Christs to one another."[7] For the most part we will perform the works of love in the ordinary sphere of our several "offices" within the orders of creation, whether as parent or child, husband or wife, prince or subject, artisan or farmer. Faith active in love expresses itself in such unspectacular feats as:

> . . . teaching the erring; comforting the afflicted; encouraging the weak; helping the neighbor in whatever way we can; bearing with his rude manners and impoliteness; putting up with annoyances, labors, and the ingratitude and contempt of men in both church and state; obeying the magistrates, treating one's parents with respect; being patient in the home with a cranky wife and an unmanageable family, and the like.[8]

It is not only in his formal writings that Luther devotes attention to the practical consequences of justification. His preaching resounds with "the call to obedience." Though the burden of his message in any sermon—whatever the text —is invariably "justification by faith," it is not uncommon for him to relate to this first and primary point a second and corollary one in which he expounds the obligations of love. Thus the story of the cleansing of the leper becomes the occasion for a sermon with two points. The leper's confidence in approaching Christ is an example of and for faith; Christ's "pure grace" in condescending to the leper's need is an example of true love for the neighbor. Thus it is shown how "faith makes of us lords, and love makes of us servants."[9]

It is clear therefore that Luther is concerned for the quality of life which faith produces. He leaves no question that good works are a consequence of grace and not its cause. He can even speak as if the new person in Christ will produce such works spontaneously, without need of commands. Nevertheless, because he views man so realistically as at once "justified and sinner" he recognizes the need for something like "the call to obedience" to incite the Christian to side with the Spirit in its continual struggle against the flesh:

> This is why faithful preachers must exert themselves as much in urging a love that is unfeigned or in urging truly

good works as in teaching true faith. Therefore, let no one think that he knows this commandment, "You shall love your neighbor," perfectly. It is very short and so far as its words are concerned, it is very easy. But show me the preachers and hearers who truly practice it in their teaching and living. I see both groups taking it easy! Thus the words, "Through love be servants of one another" and "You shall love your neighbor as yourself" are eternal words, which no one can adequately ponder, teach, and practice.[10]

## PREACHING THE CALL TO OBEDIENCE TODAY

While it is true that, from one perspective, the good works of Christians are a spontaneous overflow of the "is-ness" of their new life in Christ, from another perspective Christians stand constantly under a divine "ought" addressed to them in each concrete situation. It becomes, then, an important part of the task of preaching to clarify the nature and the content of this "ought." As did Luther in his day, the contemporary preacher will recognize the propensity of faith to become indolent unless it is incited and guided toward the works of love. Therefore the preacher will not rob his people of the direction and encouragement which they need in order to grow "to mature manhood, to the measure of the stature of the fulness of Christ . . ." (Eph. 4: 13).

Against this background we will suggest three guidelines for preaching "the call to obedience" today, offering illustrations from actual homiletical material.

1. *We will sound the call to obedience as a consequence of grace and not its cause.*

Here Luther's absolute clarity with respect to "good works" as a "fruit" rather than the foundation of justification is of central importance. In sharpest opposition to popular medieval theology which urged men to contribute to their salvation by a variety of acts of penance and obedience Luther argued—often violently—that "good works do not make a good man, but a good man does good works."[11] Grace, for Luther, is always the source of obedience, not its reward.

When in our preaching we reverse this sequence from grace to works, the sermon easily degenerates into "legalism" or "moralism." Such preaching places the imperative mood, whose appropriate function is secondary and responsory, above the indicative mood, which is always to be central and dominant in Christian proclamation. It is a telltale sign that preaching has degenerated into moralizing when the sermon is full of the verb *must* or the hortatory phrase "let us." Unless such imperatives are deeply rooted in the rich soil of the announcement of grace, they lend to the sermon a nomistic tone which negates the radical "gift" nature of the Gospel. The ultimate irony is preaching which turns even the invitation to faith into a moral demand: "We *must* have faith in God's promises" or "You *must* believe in Jesus Christ."

Here is an example of a sermon in which the imperative tends to dominate the indicative. Note the recurrence of the word *must*:

> And if we would be forgiven we must ourselves forgive. A husband said to his wife, "Come now, I thought you had agreed to forgive and forget." "Yes," she replied, "but I don't want *you* to forget that *I* have forgiven and forgotten." All of us throughout our lives, seeking forgiveness for ourselves, must extend it to others. Like electricity, if it is to have an inlet, it must have an outlet.[12]

The preacher is making an important point about the reciprocal nature of forgiveness, yet the phrasing of this passage subtly turns our forgiving behavior into a prerequisite of God's forgiving action toward us. It places upon unconditional grace a human condition and thus compromises the Gospel's radical word about God's love precisely for the ungodly and the unloving.

It would be more consistent with the nature of biblical ethics to cast the call to forgive in the indicative mood: "And as we *are* forgiven we will ourselves forgive." The true nature of Christian obedience is expressed in the sentence, "You *are*; therefore you *do*." Or, as Barth has summarized Paul's ethical stance, "Become what you are." Indeed there are Old Testament scholars who argue that the proper linguistic form of the Decalogue is indicative rather than imperative:   Because you are my people, "you *will* have no other gods before me;" "you *will* do no murder;" "you *will* not covet."[13]

No Gospel text has more traps by which a preacher can be caught in a sterile and deadening moralizing than the Sermon on the Mount.   Yet notice this passage from a Thielicke sermon entitled "No Retaliation," based on Matthew 5:38–48:

> This Jesus, who stands over there among our enviers and haters, is asking that we take our stand with him and discover the terribly ravaged sonship within our brothers and with love woo it from its grave.
> Don't you see?   This is the Gospel—with all its difficult and strange talk of loving one's enemies . . . this world which is choking and dying of hate and revenge is *waiting* for the new and renewing eyes of disciples.   It is waiting for the eyes that see man's sonship to God and *therefore* also see the bridge that leads to the neighbor's heart and even to the enemy's heart.
> That neighbor of yours who gets on your nerves—he is waiting for that look, that fellow worker with whom you are at odds, that son of yours who is breaking your heart and whom you hardly know what to do with, that husband who has changed so sadly and disappointed you so bitterly, and all the others who bring tension and discord into your life. All of them are waiting for you to discover in them what Jesus saw in them and what gave him the strength to die for them.   All of them, friends and enemies, the good and the bad, are beloved, straying, erring children of the Father in heaven who is seeking them in pain and agony.
> Who else will ever see this child of God in them and lovingly draw it out of them if not you—you who are yourself standing beneath the eyes of Jesus and being seen as such a child?[14]

Here the new ethic which governs the Christian life is

unmistakably rooted in the gracious, forgiving action of God toward us. The imperative to love grows directly out of the declaration that we are loved, and is cast—appropriately— in the indicative mood. This is not to say that we will never use the imperative mood in addressing our people with the call to obedience, but we will do so cautiously and with constant checks against any compromising of the primacy of grace.

## 2. We will articulate the call to obedience with concreteness.

Ragnar Bring has properly commented that in preaching the demand of God for our daily living "the most difficult part of it will always be to show men what the will of God really is in various concrete situations, and what it is that God asks of us."[15] All of us who preach know this. There is no difficulty in setting before our people a general call "to do justice and to love kindness." They rather expect that of us. And as we who preach, so our people who hear are easily able to avoid coming to grips with such a diffuse demand. Precisely at those points where it actually intersects our lives we all deflect and evade it. Dostoevski was right when he observed, "Love in dreams is easy; love in action is painful." Part of the burden of preaching is to be as concrete as we can about the human shape the actions of justice and love will take in a world which is often hostile to such acts.

Sometimes we try to relieve ourselves of this burden by protesting that no sermon can apply the Word to the situation of every listener in our pews. We simply never know all we need to know about the conflicting pressure under which Mrs. A is living or the complex considerations Mr. B must take into account in reaching a critical decision in his business. This is true, but we are not thereby absolved from struggling to be as concrete as possible in sounding "the call to obedience" in our preaching. Otherwise our sermons become docetic, removed from flesh-and-blood reality. They lose the cutting edge by which the Word of God cleaves to the substance of our lives.

Here again Jesus' own style of preaching can provide a model for us. When he called his listeners to a life of radical love, he did not deliver an abstract statement about the nature of love. He told the story of the Good Samaritan. Obviously, few if any of his listeners would ever find themselves in precisely the situation he described—stumbling upon a battered stranger along a remote stretch of highway. But his story provided them and us with an unforgettable paradigm of neighbor love. Now we know what such love looks like in action, and so in the quite different actualities of our own lives we cannot escape its demands.

Likewise in our own preaching of the call to obedience we must search for paradigms which will help people see with as much precision as possible the nature of the response we are asking of them. Sometimes this can be done in terms of an actual situation we know them to be facing corporately. Here, for example, is an excerpt from a sermon by Eugene Carson Blake on the parable of Dives and Lazarus. The preacher's focus is on the terrible discrepancy between the "have" and "have-not" nations:

> Recently the President asked from all the American people sacrifice and support in the face of the political and military threat to our country and to the western alliance. Congress and the people have responded with a unanimity born of well-founded fear. But at the same time there has been before Congress a new Foreign Aid Bill which languishes in committee.
>
> It is true that we cannot expect the nation made up of all kinds of believers and nonbelievers to act like a Christian Church. But may we not expect the churches in our country to act like Christian churches?
>
> Where is the flood of letters to Congress, pressing for this Bill? Where even is the informed and steady support of our own Christian programs to meet this desperate human need? . . . Where are the Christian public witnesses in plush yacht and golf clubs standing up for Christian generosity as an obligation?[16]

Sometimes the application of the call to obedience cannot relate that specifically to the majority of those who hear. But the necessity to concreteness is still upon us. One way of handling it is by means of what I would call a montage. We attempt to make some dimension of the Christian life real to our diverse listeners by flashing before them quick images of people who embody that dimension in actual life. We hope every listener will find some clue to the shape of his or her own response to a particular situation. Here is a passage in which Edmund Steimle makes use of the montage form to illustrate the strange ways in which human actions can manifest God's glory:

> There was a minister in Cleveland mightily concerned about the problem of integration in the schools who, while engaging in a public protest, got mangled to death by a bulldozer in the process. A stupid waste, I suppose. Or, there's a teacher in a classroom . . . who despite all the bureaucratic irritations, defects, and frustrations, gets a tremendous kick out of seeing to it that her kids learn to read and write and think and develop as persons. Or there's an ordinary house painter who gets tremendous satisfaction out of a job really well done. Or there's a daughter putting up with her elderly fretful mother who is convinced she has lived too long, as well as an elderly mother putting up with a fretful, impatient daughter. Or there is the student, convinced that the most crucial issue of our times is civil rights, going off to help in voter registration.[17]

Such "snapshots" of reality save the response dimension of the sermon from detachment from life. The same effect can sometimes be achieved by more extended, episodic illustrations after the fashion of the parable of the Good Samaritan, so long as they have a ring of authenticity. The danger of story illustrations is that they are often unrealistic in their portrayals of human behavior. The goal of the preacher is to "incarnate" the call to obedience as realistically as he can, to ground the appeal for a Christian life style in the recognizable relationships and dilemmas of which daily existence consists.

*3. We will point to spheres of obedience in the public as well
as the private sector.*

It is temptingly easy for us to limit the call to obedience
in our sermons to those relationships which are private and
intimate.  Most of us in our preaching find little difficulty
in delineating the ways of love in face-to-face contacts with
neighbors or within the closed circle of the family.  The
problems multiply, however, and the risks increase when we
move into the public sector and address the urgent socio-
political issues of our time.

Often we feel we do not know enough about these vast
issues to speak to them, and it is true that when we take up
a question such as world hunger or capital punishment we
need to do careful homework.  Yet the plea of ignorance
can often be a rationalization of our fear of involving ourselves in areas where the potential for conflict is high.  Our
silence may maintain a surface peace in the congregation,
but we will have bought it at the price of stifling the Word
which has power to free our people and ourselves from bondage to the myths and prejudices which hold our society in
the grip of death.

In the end, unless we are willing to retreat entirely from
the world, we can hardly avoid facing such massive problems
as war, poverty, environmental blight, and injustice to min-
orities.  Here Luther's insistence upon the secular character
of the Christian's works of love offers a foundation for our
preaching.  The Christian, in Luther's view, discovers the
obligations of his new life precisely in the sphere of his
particular "station" within the orders of creation.

It is true that in a hierarchical and authoritarian society
the forms of secular obedience seldom involved renovation
of the structures of society itself.  Our preaching context
today, however, is different.  In a participatory democracy
we enjoy at least limited leverage in the shaping of public
policy.  We will therefore help our congregations see how
the obligation to love the neighbor must often be translated

into a struggle for social justice and world peace—a struggle which involves us directly in the political realm.

Sometimes the address to public issues in our preaching will take the form of persistently raising the questions which many people would prefer to ignore. During the period of American military involvement in Southeast Asia, for example, there were those who insisted that the issues there were, in the narrowest sense, strictly military and political. Part of the task of the preacher is to keep exposing the human and, therefore, ethical concerns which underlie all other issues. Economic and geopolitical verbiage cannot be permitted to camouflage the tragic cost in pain, death and indignity exacted by war, inflation, and racial and sexual discrimination. The preacher then is the one who keeps raising the awkward questions which will prevent us from being at ease amid those forces in modern life by which people are disadvantaged and dehumanized.

This passage from another sermon on the parable of Dives and Lazarus illustrates this unsettling function of preaching:

> The picture of Dives and Lazarus is still familiar even to those of us who are living in the richest nation at the richest period of its history. At least forty million Americans receive less than the minimum income required for adequate food, clothing and shelter. One in every five Americans is poor, and half of these are children. Two thirds of the poverty group are white, although the infant mortality rate among blacks is three times higher than it is for whites. . . .
>
> To make such observations is to provoke arguments about the statistics, and in this "numbers game" the poor can easily get lost. They become digits instead of persons . . . we can fail to realize that in the shacks and tenements there are women and men who are pessimistic and fatalistic, feeling there is no way out—for themselves, or for their children, or for their grandchildren.[18]

This preacher has obviously taken time for research into the issue with which he deals, and he so utilizes his facts that we are confronted with the human dimensions of the problem of poverty. He holds the poor before us in a manner that makes it impossible for us to escape them. Later in the sermon he makes concrete suggestions about ways in which we can respond to their plight:

> We can respond to the call of Lazarus at our gate. . . . The call comes in many ways. The call comes to grapple with the issues of welfare and unemployment and to consider the public programs that can deal most constructively with these urgent needs. The call comes to join other citizens in attacking the causes of poverty and trying to break the vicious cycle that moves from father to son to grandson. The call comes to us in our place of daily work where we can train the poor and engage them in meaningful employment. The call comes to teach those who cannot read.[19]

Such preaching places heavy demands upon the industry, imagination, and integrity of the preacher. To restrict application of the call to obedience to the limited area of interpersonal relations appears simpler and easier. It is certainly safer. But the ministry of the Word is a calling whose motto might well be the slogan Johannes Hoekindijk has suggested for the whole church of Christ—"Safety Last!"[20] In the final analysis the church takes its clue from the Incarnation itself—the Gospel of One who in his crucifixion identified himself with the oppressed and miserable of the earth, and who as risen Lord leads his people toward that day in which there shall be "a new heaven and a new earth" in which righteousness dwells.

## NOTES

1. Martin Luther, "Treatise on Good Works" (1520), *LW* 44:26.

2. *LW* 44:26–27.

3. Those interested in pursuing this subject are referred to such studies as Gerhard Ebeling, "On the Doctrine *Triplex Usus Legis* in the Theology of the Reformation," and "Reflections on the Doctrine of the Law," in *Word and Faith* (Philadelphia: Fortress Press, 1960); Paul Althaus, *The Divine Command* (Philadelphia: Fortress Press, 1966); Werner Elert, *Law and Gospel* (Philadelphia: Fortress Press, 1967); Helmut Thielicke,

*Theological Ethics 1: Foundations* (Fortress Press, 1966); Wilfried Joest, *Gesetz und Freiheit* (Göttingen: Vandenhoeck & Ruprecht, 1961).

4. Martin Luther, "Lectures on Galatians" (1535), *LW* 26:350.

5. Martin Luther, "The Large Catechism," in *The Book of Concord,* ed. and trans. Theodore G. Tappert (Philadelphia: Fortress Press, 1959) p. 445.

6. Martin Luther, "Lectures on Galatians" (1535), *LW* 27:47.

7. "Hence as our Heavenly Father has in Christ freely come to our aid we also ought freely to help our neighbor through our body and its works, and each one should as it were become a Christ to the other that we may be Christs to one another and Christ be the same in all, that is that we may be truly Christians" (Martin Luther, "The Freedom of a Christian" [1520], *LW* 31:367–368).

8. *LW* 27:56.

9. Martin Luther, "Church Postil," in *Works* (Minneapolis: Lutherans in All Lands, 1906), 11:73.

10. *LW* 27:54.

11. *LW* 31:361.

12. Robert J. McCracken, "Forgiveness—Human and Divine," an unpublished sermon.

13. Jacob M. Myers, *Grace and Torah* (Philadelphia: Fortress Press, 1975), pp. 16–17.

14. Helmut Thielicke, *Life Can Begin Again* (Philadelphia: Fortress Press, 1963), pp. 78–79.

15. Ragnar Bring, "Preaching the Law," *Scottish Journal of Theology* 13 (1960): 23.

16. Eugene Carson Blake, "That Man at My Gate," *Best Sermons,* ed. G. Paul Butler (Princeton, N.J.: D. Van Nostrand Co., Inc., 1962), p. 241.

17. Edmund A. Steimle, *Disturbed by Joy* (Philadelphia: Fortress Press, 1967), p. 69.

18. Wade P. Huie, Jr., "The Poverty of Abundance," *Interpretation* 22 (1968): 405.

19. Ibid., pp. 408–409.

20. Johannes Hoekendijk, *The Church Inside Out* (Philadelphia: Westminster Press, 1966), p. 152.

# -6-

# LAW AND GOSPEL IN
# THE SERMON

Our analysis of the theological dimensions of the sermon has involved a risk: The categories of Law, Gospel, and the call to obedience, though in reality interdependent, may come to be viewed as having a relative independence of each other. They may begin to look like discrete components which need only to be inserted into the sermon at the proper place.

The risk of such a distorted view has been taken only because analysis must often arbitrarily separate elements which in reality are inseparable. Such interrelatedness pertains especially when the reality under consideration has a dynamic life of its own. This is the case with the sermon. The Word in the form of proclamation has a mysterious vitality which does not tolerate fine, sharp-boundaried differentiation of the elements of which it consists. Categories like those with which we have been dealing will always be exhibited far more precisely in a theological essay than in the actuality of preaching.

It would be a mistake, therefore, to conclude that mastery of a schematic analysis of the theological dimensions of the sermon will lead inevitably and directly to right proclamation of Law and Gospel. This might be so if a sermon were analogous, for example, to a clock. Then the proper component could be placed in the proper position in the mech-

76

anism and the clock would "go." But a sermon is not a mechanism. It is a living entity whose genesis and growth are analogous to the wondrous process by which life is conceived and then develops in the womb. The sermon's creation cannot be programmed. It is not simply a total of interchangeable parts. The dimensions of Law, Gospel, and the call to obedience move within each sermon in lively, unpredictable ways. The form of each and the shape of the whole will be as unique in every event of proclamation as with each new appearance of human life. The preacher will often be as surprised and mystified by the "being" of a sermon as is a mother when she gazes at the startling individuality of her child.

Another way of stating this point is to say that, for preaching, the conjunction in the formula "Law and Gospel" is as important as the nouns. In living proclamation we are always concerned about Law *and* Gospel. These categories live within the sermon in a dialectical relationship manifesting the same dynamic interchange as inhaling and exhaling or the coursing of blood outward from the heart through the arteries and its return through the veins. Law and Gospel are the *yin* and *yang* of the life of the Word.

THREE LIVING REALITIES IN
SERMON PREPARATION

Reflection on what we do when we prepare a sermon suggests that the process is an interplay of three living realities— the Word, the congregation, and the preacher. Perhaps better, the preacher provides the living matrix in which the other two realities meet in highly volatile interchange. The preacher both hosts that interchange and conditions it. Each sermon with its particular Law/Gospel configuration is a fourth living reality generated by the other three.

*The Word of Scripture*

Among these realities the Word must be first both in position and in authority. Of the sermon too it must be said,

"In the beginning was the Word. . . ." Preaching which is
not rooted in and nourished by Scripture—what Barth calls
"the second form of the Word of God"—is, in terms of the
central tradition of the church, deviant. It is assumed therefore that the preparation of the sermon will begin with serious attentiveness to a text.

As preachers we will actively "listen" for many things in
the text—its form, its linguistic structure, its referents to a
history outside itself—but we will listen for nothing more
intently than for the dominant accent with which it speaks,
whether of Law or Gospel. Does this text utter a judgment
which throws our life and that of our culture under radical
question? Does it evoke some poignant aspect of our alienated humanity—loneliness, anxiety, hopelessness? Does it
resound with some liberating word of affirmation and promise? Does it lay upon us some inexorable demand growing
out of God's own unconditional and indescribable generosity?
Some texts will bid us answer "Yes" to all of those questions.
Others will speak more loudly with only one accent. As
preachers we will pray for sensitivity to hear the characteristic Word of each text, and for integrity and skill to allow
that Word to dominate the sermon we preach.

Such attentive listening will save us from imposing our
own predisposition upon the text. My experience and ob-
servation teach me that our almost unalterable bias is for
Law at the expense of Gospel. I know first hand that it is
possible for a preacher to distort the luminous promises of
the Beatitudes into a crushing burden of demand that people
be meek, righteous, and peaceable. I have also heard a sermon transmute the Johannine story of Jesus' free, prevenient,
life-giving action upon Lazarus into a stern requirement that
*we* remove the "stones" of doubt and disobedience that keep
us enclosed in our world of death!

Even when a text seems to be in itself wholly Law or
Gospel, the actual sermon will not be without its counter
dimension. For one thing, the total biblical witness is the
wider context of each individual lection and cannot be

ignored when we preach. Furthermore, we cannot make the Gospel credible in our preaching without at least some indication of our awareness of those aspects of the human situation to which it speaks. And surely no preacher whose mandate springs directly from the Good News of Jesus' death and resurrection will proclaim what appears to be a text's total Word of judgment or demand without letting God's "No" against our human way be heard in dialectical relationship with the still more powerful "Yes" of his grace. In short, while respecting the dominating Word of the text, our homiletical articulation of that Word will reflect the fact that Law and Gospel are the twofold form of the one Word spoken by the one God and Father of all. Whatever their balance in a particular sermon, both Law and Gospel will, almost without exception, be present.

*The Congregation*

The other living reality which affects the relational stresses among the theological dimensions of a particular sermon is the congregation in its concrete situation. A sermon is never an abstraction prepared for a nameless, faceless audience. A sermon is a historical event; that is, it occurs in a particular setting in time and space and can be divorced from that setting only at the cost of a loss in reality. For sermons, as for other living organisms, uprooting is perilous. This is why a printed sermon read by someone who is a stranger to the original preaching situation loses the force of the firsthand event of proclamation. There is no substitute for a living preacher among living hearers.

This historical setting of the actual congregation conditions many aspects of the sermon—vocabulary, illustration, design, and not least the handling of Law, Gospel, and the call to obedience. Notice that the verb used in the preceding sentence is "conditions" and not "determines." Only the Word in the text is in a determinative position with respect to the fundamental message of the sermon. Yet, just as the Word in the form of the Incarnate One did not disregard the realities of a given historical time and place, so the Word in preaching will be responsive to the actual configurations of life within the congregation. Such factors as the socioeconomic situation of the congregation, the political realities impinging upon the people at a particular time, or public events in which they are caught up will condition the way Law and Gospel themes sound in a particular sermon.

If, for example, the sermon text is Isaiah 40 with its powerful call to "Comfort, comfort" the people, the sermon surely will emerge differently in a congregation of the dispossessed in the ghetto than in a congregation of the affluent in the suburbs. In the first instance, the identification between the listeners—alienated from the "good life" of society and oppressed by its structures—and the exiles in Babylon will be immediate and direct. The preacher will need to exert only limited effort in establishing the need of his people for "comfort." The Law will be preached as a description of their existence, a gentle reminder of "man's being as it in fact is." The burden of the sermon will be to proclaim the graciousness of the God who does not forget his people in affliction but works in history for their deliverance.

In a congregation of the affluent, who are themselves part of the structures of oppression, the same approach would be impossible. At one level, the very security of the people obscures a sense of need and makes the proclamation of "comfort to the afflicted" meaningless. Homiletical stress in such a situation may need to fall much more heavily upon the later word in this passage which undercuts the reliability of all earthly securities: "All flesh is grass, and all its beauty is like the flower of the field" (Isa. 40:6). Yet preachers of the Gospel will not allow such necessary judgment to obliterate the Word of God's promise which reaches out to our people without exception. We will be aware of the fact that loneliness and despair are not phenomena to be found only among the poor and oppressed of the earth but that they take their own poignant form even among those who may appear to have cause only to rejoice.

*The Preacher*

Finally, we must turn to the third living reality—the host of the dynamic interchange between text and context, pericope and people. It is from within our consciousness as preachers that the sermon is generated. In our own being we provide the womb for the birth of a new form of the Word of God.

To think of each Sunday's sermon in just this way heightens the awe and expectation with which we enter upon our weekly task. There will be awe, because nothing less than God's Word for the present moment will be struggling for life in and through our words. There will be expectation, because none other than the Holy Spirit is at work in the process out of which a sermon is born.

It would not be sacrilegious for us when we begin our preparation for preaching to offer the prayer of Mary in response to the Annunciation: "Behold, I am the [servant] of the Lord; let it be to me according to your word" (Luke 1:38). An analogous and mysterious appropriation of the human by the divine is present in the creation of a sermon. Preaching, in short, is in some sense "incarnational." The Word makes use of our "flesh"—limited, flawed, vulnerable as it is—to engage humanity in the present hour.

To speak of preaching as "incarnational" is not to deify or spiritualize it but rather to underscore its humanity. The sermon does not inhabit that eternal, ineffable realm where God dwells in unapproachable glory and where his Word is present in undivided unity. The sermon is an event in history where the Word of God resounds in the dialectic of Law and Gospel. When we preach, we speak the Word in this twofold form. It is for this reason that we must cultivate the capacity to reflect on the theological motifs which reach expression in our sermons.

To stress the "incarnational" nature of preaching suggests also that as preachers we are far more than inert hosts of the interchange between the two realities of text and congregation. As noted earlier, we condition as well as host that interchange. God willingly takes the risk of placing the treasure of his Word in "earthen vessels" (2 Cor. 4:7). Though we pray that the Word may have "free course" in our proclamation, for better or for worse that Word is always subject to the partialness of our understanding, the limitations of our knowledge, the biases of our attitudes, and the resistance and rebelliousness of our egos. Every time we preach, the Word must triumph over us as well as employ us.

This fact makes our preparation for preaching as much a battle scene as a birth process. Strife as well as labor is present. I once heard our weekly encounter with the Word compared with Jacob's midnight wrestling match against his terrifying adversary at the brook Jabbok. The analogy is not overdrawn. Each week our calling to preach plunges us into the pit with the Word of God. Of necessity we are laid open to engagement with the Word as Law and Gospel. The outcome may be no more clear for us than it was for Jacob. We will carry away psychic marks of our struggles analogous to his crippled thigh. So far as I can see, this weekly duty to wrestle with the Word as we prepare to preach is the only possible advantage we clergy have over the laity of the church. Unless we only feign engagement, we cannot escape that regular exposure to Law and Gospel in which we are both wounded and healed.

What I am struggling to communicate is the fact that our preparation to preach is itself the process by which Law and Gospel become more than abstract theological principles. Our places of study become arenas in which we ourselves are grasped by those categories as by living hands. Here we are seized by a knowledge that there is no escaping, namely, that our failures in love and our disloyalties to truth are as profound and pervasive as those of any person to whom we preach. Here is stripped away the superficial covering beneath which we usually manage to hide the loneliness, the emptiness, the anxiousness, and the instabilities which gnaw at the core of our lives. Here the Word of our free and unconditional acceptance, which nothing but our inveterate pride can keep us from hearing, is spoken again and again. Here we are drawn into relationship with that imperishable Reality which is the true center underlying and renewing the constantly threatened center of our own being. Here we are beckoned toward patterns of self-discipline and self-giving which, left to ourselves, we would summarily reject even if they were to occur to us. Thus, in our preparation to preach, Law and Gospel move from being categories by which we think to becoming realities out of which we live. If this does not happen to us during the hours of preparation, it is unlikely that it will happen to our people during the minutes of our proclamation.

## A JOURNAL
## OF TWO ENCOUNTERS

It may be that the dialectic I have been attempting to describe throughout this book, but especially in this closing chapter, will be served best by concrete example. I invite you, therefore, to come with me into the arena and join me vicariously in my encounter with the Word of God as it struggled for expression in two preaching texts. I will try as best I can to recover something of the process by which the themes of Law, Gospel, and call to obedience took shape for me in two actual sermons. As my companion and critic you will have to judge whether the decisions made along the way were faithful to the text and appropriate to the preaching context.

As to context, the first of the two sermons was prepared for preaching in what is now my most regular congregation— a seminary community. The occasion was a eucharistic service during the first week in Advent. The second sermon was prepared for a more typical local congregation and grew out of an exegetical study I was doing at the time on Matthew's version of the Lord's Prayer.

### Encounter I

Actually, I found myself engaged with three texts as I prepared for the Advent preaching assignment. The first two—

Isaiah 63:16–17; 64:1–8 and I Corinthians 1:3–9—were appointed by a lectionary. The third—Mark 11:1–10—was selected because it relates an event traditionally held before the church as Advent begins. The Isaiah text begins with one of the few affirmations of God as "Father" in the Old Testament. It then moves on to the heart-wrenching plea of a disillusioned people for God to "rend the heavens and come down" as he had in ancient times for their deliverance. The passage from 1 Corinthians contains Paul's thanksgiving for God's spiritual gifts poured out upon the troublesome congregation in Corinth and his assurance to them that "God is faithful." The Markan text is that gospel's version of the Palm Sunday entrance into Jerusalem.

An initial reading of these lessons began to establish the Isaiah passage in my mind as the primary preaching text. This may have been in part because Advent is for me a season in which Old Testament texts speak with special power. It is a season of longing and expectation, of hope yet to be fulfilled. The prophets, with their polarities of dismay about the present and confidence for the future, are the preeminent spokesmen of this Advent mood. They remind us in the church that, though we live in the light of Jesus' death and resurrection there is always a "not yet" about our life in history. Texts such as this passage from Isaiah can prevent us from making the unwarranted leap into supposed eschatological fulfillment about which Bonhoeffer warned: "In my opinion it is not Christian to want to take our thoughts and feelings too quickly and too directly from the New Testament."[1]

With the decision made to preach primarily on the Isaiah text, I began exegetical study of this passage. I was reminded that the voice we hear in these verses is that of "Third Isaiah" speaking to those who had returned from exile in Babylon. But the return, desired for so many years and promised so eloquently by "Second Isaiah," had not brought fulfillment. "Third Isaiah" prophesied in what could be described as the "dog days" of Israel's history. Though many years had passed since the return, Jerusalem was still a desolation and the temple rubble.  People were saying out loud that the lush gardens they knew in Babylon were to be preferred to the dusty waste which now surrounded them.  It is clear then that the prophet is speaking for a people who felt trapped in a dreary, disillusioned time.  "O that thou wouldst rend the heavens and come down and make the heavens tremble before thee" is part prayer and part cry of despair.

It was here that the text suddenly began to lay hold of me. I found the prophet speaking for me as much as for Israel. His cry echoed voices I had heard sounding in my own consciousness and from the consciousness of my contemporaries.  To put it in the categories we have been using, the Word in this text began to speak powerfully for me as Law under the aspect of the "mirror of existence."  Life as it is— not as I would like it to be—was being reflected back to me.

What I saw in the mirror of this text was existence cast in the image of the trap or the dead end.  The text forced me to reflect upon those times when in personal affairs or in the larger dynamics of our society circumstances so close in upon us that all visible openings into the future are blocked. God remains silent.  All the promises on which we had counted appear to have been voided.  The only prospect is "tomorrow, tomorrow, and tomorrow" in unchanging defeat.

And yet in a strange way this bleak, "Lawish" mood began already to function for me as Gospel.  At one level, the very fact that these words from an ancient prophet were speaking *for* me as well as *to* me broke into my isolation.  Others, it was clear, had known the bitter taste of despair, and by giving it open expression before God had become my companions in the trap-like conditions of my own life and time. Indeed it was as though God were affirming my right not to hide from the potentially most destructive realities in and around my existence.  To know despair was not to be wrong but to be human.

At another level, the anguished cry of the prophet that God

might "rend the heavens and come down" began to make itself heard as the voice of unextinguishable "hope against hope." Born from despair, it spoke nevertheless of faith. Here was the paradox of our human hearts pleading with the God whom we feel at the same moment to be deaf to our prayers. To the God who seems to be either indifferent or impotent we continue to cry out our own versions of Isaiah's prayer: "Act, God, act! Not just in history in general, not just in history past—but in *our* history, *now!*"

Thus a text which helped expose "the dark underside" of our existence, functioning thereby as a word of Law, already began to speak with liberating accents by inviting me into solidarity with all who know what it is to be caught in circumstances over which they have lost control. One preaching goal with respect to this text, therefore, became that of evoking from my listeners a similar recognition of the currents of hopelessness which ran through their own responses to life.

Important as this aspect of the text was in opening a way into the human situation to be addressed, it actually provided only the minor theme of the sermon, and in terms of quantity of material only a brief segment. Far more important for the message to be preached were the voices of hope which kept weaving in and out of Isaiah's lamentations:

> . . . thou, O Lord art our Father,
> our Redeemer from of old is thy name. (63:16)

> When thou didst terrible things
> which we looked not for,
>    thou camest down,
> the mountains quaked at thy presence. (64:3)

> Yet, O Lord, thou art our Father;
>    we are the clay, and thou art the potter;
> we are all the work of thy hand. (64:8)

Here the desperate yearnings voiced in 64:1 are answered by ringing assurances that God has not abandoned his people. He is the one who *has* "come down" and accomplished on behalf of his chosen people such "terrible things" that even the mountains shudder before him.  Such a God can be counted on to act in the present and in the future.

But the questions which forced themselves urgently upon me were "How?" and "Where?"  The references in 64:3 were probably to the thunderings and lightnings which accompanied God's epiphany to Moses on Mt. Sinai.  Such imagery, however, is not apt to carry much meaning for a contemporary congregation.  We are not apt to look to upheavals in nature for the signs of God's intervention in our affairs.  Yet both this text and the motifs of the Advent season were generating for me a sense of anticipation that God does and will act for our good, a hope that he is neither locked up in ancient centuries nor sealed off somewhere in "the heavens."  The traditional Advent collect, "Stir up, we beseech thee, thy power, O Lord, and come" is one which the church prays with confidence—that again in our own times and circumstances he *will* come.  How then to articulate this Gospel word of hope in a way that would give it some chance of being heard?  This became the major problem with which I had to struggle.

It was at this point that the texts from Mark's gospel and the letter to the Corinthians gave me help.  Especially read in juxtaposition with Isaiah's word about a God who does such "terrible things" that the mountains quake, the Markan account of Jesus' entry into Jerusalem was instructive.  Here is a record of God acting in history for our good.  This is what it looks like, the evangelist seems to be saying, when God comes to his people to open a way for them.  Our King comes as a peasant riding a donkey.  Actually, the whole scene appears to be written as a deliberate parody of all invasions of cities that have ever been—a carpet of cast-off clothing instead of bombs, the singing of children rather than the thunder of artillery, palm fronds instead of bayonets.  The episode began to emerge for me as having an almost ludicrous quality.  I sensed the legitimacy of modern portrayals of Jesus as a clown—the court jester of the kingdom of heaven who pokes holes in all earthly pretensions of power.

Though this perspective obviously brings with it an element of judgment upon our society's obsession with bigness and force, the Palm Sunday story came home to me chiefly as a clue to where to look for God's interventions in history. It suggested to me that our understanding of Isaiah's word "terrible" needed revising. I began to see that what ultimately has power in the world isn't force that can be measured in megatons, or authority which sits in high places, but rather realities which in our human eyes are apt to seem utterly impotent, absolutely vulnerable, and ludicrously insignificant.

Here the stories surrounding the nativity which the church reads at the end of the Advent season reenforced Mark's account of Palm Sunday. What could be more impotent, vulnerable, and apparently insignificant than a baby? And yet the first reverberations of the hidden power at the heart of such apparent powerlessness can be seen in Matthew's story of Herod's panicked slaughter of the infants of Bethlehem. Thus in a way Isaiah could not have foreseen it is true that "when thou didst terrible things that we did not look for [like assuming the vulnerability of infant flesh and blood], the mountains shuddered before thee." In this babe in a manger, this peasant on a donkey, this dead man on a cross was hidden the power which has been able to shake the nations and shape history.

This clue as to the strange places where we should look for God's intervening activity led me to reflect upon some of the unlikely forms in which he comes to us today. Here the text from 1 Corinthians was helpful. As I reread it in the light of the insight gained from the Markan lesson, what Paul was saying struck me as absolutely astonishing. He was expressing joyous thanksgiving for the "grace of God" which had poured out such a plenitude of spiritual gifts upon the Corinthian church. *This* to a congregation he is about to blast with charges of divisiveness, outrageous immorality,

and assorted other violations of all that the Gospel means!
Yet Paul is sure that in this motley, unfaithful, unlikely collection of people the Spirit is busy, because as he puts it
"God is faithful." Here again is the promise disclosed in
the Palm Sunday narrative, that God chooses for his points
of entry into the world those persons, groups, and events
which from the human perspective are apt to seem most
unlikely.

For me this was a shining word of Gospel. It assured me
that God does not require superior material or promising
circumstances to accomplish his purposes. I heard in a new
way the meaning of Isaiah's familiar words, "We are the
clay, and thou art the potter" (64:8). God is able to take
up the most ordinary and unimpressive material and shape
it to his design. As Nikos Kazantzakēs once put it, if God is
indeed a potter then it must follow that "he works with
mud."² Here was an opportunity to articulate God's affirmation of us all, standing before him as we always do at some
level of our lives, broken, confused, hopeless. The texts
were saying to me, as I would try to say to the congregation,
that God acts more often at the point of our most painful
defeats than at the point of our supposed victories. All of
this was brought into christological focus for me when the
momentum of the texts led me to reflect upon how, on the
day when above all days God rent the heavens and "came
down" terrible in love, it was by way of a man who had
hung powerless on a cross and had been laid lifeless in a
tomb.

This "journal of an encounter" scarcely suggests the form
into which the actual sermon was finally shaped for preaching. As it happens, the rhythm of thought about the texts
was generally repeated in the structure of the sermon. The
sermon moved basically from the preaching of Law as "mirror
of existence" to a proclamation of Gospel as "antiphon to
existence." The pairing of Law and Gospel in this case
might be described as despair/hope or impotence/possibility.
The division, however, was not neatly Point I—Law, Point

II—Gospel. As has been noted, the clarification of the human situation in the Isaiah text already began to introduce nuances of Gospel by drawing us into the community of the distressed. Likewise, the Gospel word that God intervenes most powerfully in and through the humanly powerless speaks implicitly a word of judgment against the mistaken identifications of power we usually make. In this sermon the call to obedience never came to explicit expression. That motif was not present in direct form in the texts, and as the sermon developed structurally it seemed to me that to introduce it would have meant an arbitrary intrusion on the dominating theme. Here is a case where one hopes that the liberating affirmation of the Gospel will give people new freedom to act when and where action is possible.

*Encounter II*

As indicated above, the second sermon whose development I will trace was prepared for a more typical congregational setting. The text for it is Matthew 6:9, the opening address of the Lord's Prayer: "Our Father who art in heaven." I had been engaged in an exegetical study of the whole prayer in Matthew's setting and, because of some of the fundamental issues raised by its opening words, decided to prepare a sermon on just that portion.

What arrested my attention was this invocation's simple affirmation of the fatherliness of God. I was suddenly struck by the difficulty—even the impossibility—of making that utterly trustful statement today. Natural and historical phenomena make it audacious, not to say absurd, to name the universe a home where we are related to God as children to a father.

Paradoxically therefore, just as the cry of despair in the Isaiah text functioned in part for me as Gospel so this beautifully clear Gospel-bearing affirmation began to function for me as Law. That is, it exposed the gnawing doubts which always accompany my verbalizations of faith. I was forced to reflect on the fact that even those of us who pray

these familiar words with great regularity often do not do
so with full confidence that we are talking to or about someone real. In the age of "the absence of God," it becomes
increasingly difficult for people to believe that in some cosmic
sense we live in a home where we're known and cared for
by an invisible, all-powerful, all-loving Father. More and
more, people feel like orphans cut adrift in space.

This mood was one I recognized in my own consciousness
and knew to be present for many who would be listening to
me. For some this doubt, which is always the shadowy companion of faith, would be subconscious. It seemed to me
that at this point it might be helpful to speak *for* my listeners, bringing into the light of day where it could be dealt
with the unbelief which is a portion of our common humanity. Law would function at this stage of the sermon as
"mirror of existence," but it would also, I hoped, have a
cathartic effect for those in whom doubt was suppressed.
Here again is an instance of a principle enunciated in Chapter 1, that Law and Gospel, though subject to separation in
theological analysis, often interpenetrate each other in actual
sermons, and certainly in human experience.

Why, I asked myself, is belief in the fatherliness of God
such a problem for us today? I decided that beyond the
problem of God itself there are at least two roots to our
difficulty. The first is our radically changed conception of
the universe. For Jesus and his contemporaries, living in a
relatively compact three-story cosmos, the imagery of father-
child did not involve quite as incredible a stretch of sensi-
bility as for us. We must live with the knowledge of a universe in which stars and galaxies by the trillions spin through
space that has no known limits. The sense of intimacy en-
gendered by the analogical language of home and family
seems utterly incongruous with the immensity of which we
are such infinitesimal parts. The scope of the universe
known to us today breeds within us a sense of being castaways
in space, orphans in the vastness of the cosmos.

It seemed to me, however, that the second root of our

difficulty is still more serious and certainly not peculiar to our modern consciousness. The universe seems not only too large to be a home but also too cruel. The problem of suffering which plagued the author of Job and which receives no rational resolution anywhere in the biblical literature is still our chief barrier against affirming a God who knows us and cares for us like a father. How can pain continue to throb through the universe if its Creator and Ruler is also like a father who loves and cares for us as his children? *Could* not one who is so all-powerful as to be named "God" remove suffering? And *would* not one who is so all-loving as to be called "Father" will to do so? I found my reflections taking me back to Albert Camus' powerful novel, *The Plague*, in which a courageous and humane physician fighting a desperate battle to minister to a city stricken by bubonic plague declares, "Until my dying day I shall refuse to love a scheme of things in which children are put to the torture."[3] That rebellious cry, it seemed to me, put into words our own most honest thoughts when confronted with inexplicable pain.

The Gospel offers no intellectual solution to these questions which rise in our hearts concerning the fatherliness of God. It rather proclaims a message which invites us to a response of faith even while our questions persist. Fundamentally, that message is the word of the cross. The reality of God's caring love is not a truth we extrapolate from the facts of nature or the general course of world history. In both nature and history there is always at least as much to contradict that reality as to affirm it. The knowledge that fathering love is the secret of the universe is a truth of revelation received only by faith, and the revelation of that love has its center point in Jesus' death and resurrection.

There needed to be in the sermon therefore some way of speaking about Jesus as the embodiment of the very prayer of faith he was teaching his disciples, some movement toward a christological statement concerning God's fatherliness. I decided it would be consistent with the developing theme of the sermon to do this in analogical language still drawn from the realm of the family. The church has often spoken of Jesus as the "elder brother" among those who are incorporated into the family of God. I found a contemporary symbol for this ancient designation in the recollection of an article about a search conducted by an older brother for an American pilot shot down over the Vietnamese jungle. I could not remember whether the search had been successful. The important thing, however, was the fact that this older brother had been a walking, searching, suffering demonstration of the fact that the lost pilot was not abandoned. He was followed by love into the depths of the jungle. He had a home.

This, it seemed to me, offered a way of speaking about one aspect of the significance of the incarnation. Jesus is like an "elder brother," the Son come from the Father's house as a sign that we are never abandoned. He is a walking, searching, suffering demonstration of a love which follows us to the extremities of our existence and participates in our suffering. This brother man on his cross, crying out of anguish and darkness to the God who appeared to have forsaken him, is the partner of our pain. His resurrection becomes the vindication of his faith and ours. Nothing in his death and resurrection resolves the intellectual problem of suffering. He offers rather the certitude that no matter how immense the universe may seem there is a love at its heart that is vaster still. And no matter how cruel the universe may seem there is a love at its heart that takes the pain upon itself—a God who is "the Great Companion, the fellow sufferer who understands."[4]

My goal in this section of the sermon was to articulate the Gospel in a way that responded to the aspects of reality set forth in the earlier section. It should be emphasized again that this reality of our doubt-filled, pain-streaked existence was itself raised as a problem by the text's affirmation of God's fathering love. I hoped too that persistence with the imagery of familial relationships would humanize the theological points being made. It was also my intention to avoid any suggestion that suffering can be bypassed in our life in history. I tried to preserve the "in the midst of" quality which must always accompany the preaching and hearing of the promise.

In retrospect I believe I could have ended the sermon at this point. No doubt it would have been sufficient to try to speak to and for my listeners about the roots of our unbelief and to make some attempt to share with them a way in which I heard the Gospel speaking to our human condition. The result would have been a bipolar Law/Gospel sermon. At the time, however, I decided to deal with the category we have called "the call to obedience."

What led me to this step was the thought that just as Jesus in his suffering, risen humanity is the sign, planted at the center of history, of God's father-love, so the church as his body is to serve as the continuing sign of that love. It occurred to me that one way of speaking about the mission of the church and the calling of every Christian is to say that we are to help close the credibility gap which continues to make it difficult for people to believe. Christian witness really means serving the possibility that persons who no longer can will once again be able to pray, "Our Father. . . ."

These reflections led me into a brief section of the sermon in which Law as the "hammer of judgment" fell with some weight. To describe the Christian calling as I have done above is also to expose the fact that we have been deficient in its accomplishment. Indeed, we have sometimes added to the difficulties people already have in believing that this universe is in some sense a home fathered by one who knows and cares. Later petitions in the Lord's Prayer itself suggested ways in which this happens, for example, our grudging sharing of "daily bread" with the world's hungry and the vindictiveness we often manifest toward those who need our forgiveness.

My purpose, however, was not to shame people into some new forms of obedience but rather to attract them to the prospect of literally "re-presenting" the love of God to persons now alienated from it. Again it seemed important to stay within the imagery of family life. I attempted to create for the listeners a vision of themselves as brothers and sisters within the family of God who are called to extend the bounds of their household of faith to include others. I tried to root this call in the reality of grace by referring again to what has been revealed to us by the action of Jesus, the "elder brother" of us all. Just as he has made it possible for us to pray, "Our Father . . .," so we will assist those desolate, lonely people who cry out into the immensity that surrounds them but hear nothing in return beyond the echo of their own voices. For all those now under the illusion that they are orphans in the universe, we will become "little Christs"—living signs that for them too there is a Father and a home.

## NOTES

1. Dietrich Bonhoeffer, *Letters and Papers from Prison* (New York: The Macmillan Company, 1972), p. 157.

2. Nikos Kazantzakēs, *The Greek Passion* (New York: Simon and Schuster, 1965), p. 151.

3. Albert Camus, *The Plague* (New York: Random House, 1948), pp. 196–197.

4. Alfred North Whitehead, *Process and Reality* (New York: The Macmillan Company, 1929), p. 532.